JUST MY TYPE

JUST MY TYPE

A book about fonts   Simon Garfield

P

PROFILE BOOKS

By the same author

The End of Innocence
The Wrestling
The Nation's Favourite
Mauve
The Last Journey of William Huskisson
Our Hidden Lives
We are at War
Private Battles
The Error World
Mini
Exposure

www.simongarfield.com

To Ben and Jake

The main chapters of this book are typeset in Sabon MT 11/15pt. Sabon, a traditional serif font, was developed in the 1960s by Jan Tschichold, a Leipzig based designer. Its story is told on p 251. Interspersed with the chapters are a series of 'FontBreaks', which are set in Univers 45 Light 9.5/15pt, except for their initial paragraphs, which appear in the font under discussion. Univers is a Swiss font, designed in 1957, the same year as its compatriot, Helvetica. Their story is told in *Chapter Nine: What is is about the Swiss?* But, being a book about fonts, *Just My Type* also samples more than 200 other fonts, from Albertus to Zeppelin II.

Design, layout and font wrangling by James Alexander of Jade Design (www.jadedesign.co.uk).

First published in 2010 by
Profile Books, 3A Exmouth House
Pine Street, Exmouth Market
London, EC1R OJH

Printed and bound in Great Britain
by T.J. International
on Forest Stewardship Council
(mixed sources) certified paper.

 **Mixed Sources**
Product group from well-managed
forests and other controlled sources
www.fsc.org Cert no. SGS-COC-2482
© 1996 Forest Stewardship Council

352pp

A catalogue record for this book is
available from the British Library.
ISBN 978-1846683015
eISBN 978-1847652928

In Budapest, surgeons operated on printer's apprentice Gyoergyi Szabo, 17, who, brooding over the loss of a sweetheart, had set her name in type and swallowed the type.

Time magazine, 28 December 1936

Contents

Introduction

Love Letters

On 12th June 2005, a fifty-year-old man stood up in front of a crowd of students at Stanford University and spoke of his campus days at a lesser institution, Reed College in Portland, Oregon. 'Throughout the campus,' he remembered, 'every poster, every label on every drawer, was beautifully hand calligraphed. Because I had dropped out and didn't have to take the normal classes, I decided to take a calligraphy class to learn how to do this. I learned about serif and sans serif typefaces, about varying the amount of space between different letter combinations, about what makes great typography great. It was beautiful, historical, artistically subtle in a way that science can't capture, and I found it fascinating.'

At the time, the student drop-out believed that nothing he had learned would find a practical application in his life. But things changed. Ten years after college, that man, by the name of Steve Jobs, designed his first Macintosh computer, a machine that came with something unprecedented – a wide choice of fonts. As well as including familiar types such as Times New Roman and Helvetica, Jobs introduced several new designs, and had evidently taken some care in their appearance and names. They were called after cities he loved such as Chicago and Toronto. He wanted each of them to be as distinct and beautiful as the calligraphy he had encountered a decade before, and at least two of the fonts, Venice and Los Angeles, had a handwritten look to them.

It was the beginning of something – a seismic shift in our everyday relationship with letters and with type. An innovation that, within a decade or so, would place the word 'font' – previously a piece of technical language limited to the design and printing trade – in the vocabulary of every computer user.

You can't easily find Jobs's original typefaces these days, which may be just as well: they are coarsely pixelated and cumbersome to manipulate. But the ability to change fonts at all seemed like technology from another planet. Before the Macintosh of 1984, primitive computers offered up one dull face, and good luck trying to italicize it. But now there was a choice of alphabets that did their best to recreate something we were used to from the real world. The chief among them was **Chicago**, which Apple used for all its menus and dialogs on screen, right through to the early iPods. But you could also opt for old black letters that resembled the work of Chaucerian scribes (𝔏𝔬𝔫𝔡𝔬𝔫), clean Swiss letters that reflected corporate modernism (Geneva), tall and airy letters that could have graced the menus of ocean liners (New York). There was even San Francisco, a font that looked as if it had been torn from newspapers – useful for tedious school projects and ransom notes.

IBM and Microsoft would soon do their best to copy Apple's lead, while domestic printers (a novel concept at the time) began to be marketed not only on speed but for the variety of their fonts. These days the concept of 'desktop publishing' conjures up a world of dodgy party invitations and soggy community magazines, but it marked a glorious freedom from the tyranny of professional typesetters and the frustrations of rubbing a sheet of Letraset. A personal change of typeface really said something: a creative move towards expressiveness, a liberating playfulness with words.

And today we can imagine no simpler everyday artistic freedom than that pull-down font menu. Here is the spill of history, the echo of Johannes Gutenberg with every key tap. Here are names we recognize: Helvetica, Times New Roman, Palatino and Gill Sans. Here are the names from folios and flaking manuscripts: Bembo, Baskerville and Caslon. Here are possibilities for flair: Bodoni, Didot and Book Antiqua. And here are the risks of ridicule: Brush Script, Herculanum

Chicago on an early iPod

and Braggadocio. Twenty years ago we hardly knew them, but now we all have favourites. Computers have rendered us all gods of type, a privilege we could never have anticipated in the age of the typewriter.

Yet when we choose Calibri over Century, or the designer of an advertisement picks Centaur rather than Franklin Gothic, what lies behind our choice and what impression do we hope to create? When we choose a typeface, what are we really saying? Who makes these fonts and how do they work? And just why do we need so many? What are we to do with Alligators, Accolade, Amigo, Alpha Charlie, Acid Queen, Arbuckle, Art Gallery, Ashley Crawford, Arnold Böcklin, Andreena, Amorpheus, Angry and Anytime Now? Or Banjoman, Bannikova, Baylac, Binner, Bingo, Blacklight, Blippo or Bubble Bath? (And how lovely does Bubble Bath sound, with its thin floating linked circles ready to pop and dampen the page?)

There are more than 100,000 fonts in the world. But why can't we keep to a half-dozen or so – perhaps familiar faces

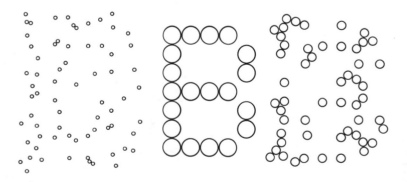

Bubble Bath – light, regular and bold

like Times New Roman, Helvetica, Calibri, Gill Sans, Frutiger or Palatino? Or the classic Garamond, named after the type designer Claude Garamond, active in Paris in the first half of the sixteenth century, whose highly legible roman type blew away the heavy fustiness of his German predecessors, and later, adapted by William Caslon in England, would provide the letters for the American Declaration of Independence.

Typefaces are now 560 years old. So when a Brit called Matthew Carter constructed Verdana and Georgia on his computer in the 1990s, what could he possibly be doing to an A and a B that had never been done before? And how did a friend of his make the typeface **Gotham**, which eased Barack Obama into the Presidency? And what exactly makes a font presidential or American, or British, French, German, Swiss or Jewish?

These are arcane mysteries and it is the job of this book to get to the heart of them. But we should begin with a cautionary tale, a story of what happens when a typeface gets out of control.

We don't serve your type

1

A duck walks into a bar and says, 'I'll have a beer please!' And the barman says, 'Shall I put it on your bill?'

How funny is that? Quite funny. The first time you heard it. It's the sort of joke you can remember – one that shows people you are not totally unable to tell a joke. A joke that a child can tell, or an uncle. The sort of joke that if you saw it on a greetings card would appear – as it does above – in **Comic Sans**.

Even if you didn't know what it was called, you will be familiar with Comic Sans. It looks as if it was written neatly by an eleven-year-old: smooth and rounded letters, nothing unexpected, the sort of shape that could appear in alphabet soup or as magnets on fridges, or in Adrian Mole's diary. If you see a word somewhere with each letter in a different colour, that word is usually in Comic Sans.

Comic Sans is type that has gone wrong. It was designed with strict intentions by a professional man with a solid philosophical grounding in graphic arts, and it was unleashed upon the world with a kind heart. It was never intended to cause revulsion or loathing, much less end up (as it has) on the side of an ambulance or a gravestone. It was intended to be fun. And, oddly enough, it was never intended to be a typeface at all.

The man to blame – although you wouldn't be the first to do so, and he takes any criticism with a genial shrug of his shoulders – is Vincent Connare. In 1994, Connare sat at his computer terminal and started to think that he could improve the human condition. Most good type starts out this way. In Connare's case, he wanted to fix a problem his employers had stumbled into without thinking.

Connare worked at Microsoft Corporation. He joined not long after the company had started to dominate the digital world, but before it became known as the Evil Empire. His job title was not 'font designer', for that might have implied some sort of old-world arts-and-crafts chair whittler, but 'typographic engineer'. He had arrived from Agfa/Compugraphic, where he worked on many type designs, some of them licensed to Microsoft's rival, Apple, and had trained first as a photographer and painter.

One day early in 1994, Connare looked at his computer screen and saw something strange. He was clicking his way through an unreleased trial copy of Microsoft Bob, a software package designed to be particularly user-friendly. It included a finance manager and a word processor, and for a time was the responsibility of Melinda French, who later became Mrs Bill Gates.

Connare spotted that there was one thing particularly wrong with Bob: its typeface. The instructions, designed in accessible language and with appealing illustrations (designed, in fact, for people who might otherwise be scared of computers), were set in Times New Roman. This looked ugly, because the software was warm and fuzzy and held your hand, while Times New Roman was traditional and chilly. It appeared an even stranger choice when paired with the child-friendly illustrations that accompanied it, not least of Bob himself – a waggy, sweet-talking dog.

Connare suggested to Microsoft Bob's designers that his experience of working with the company's educational and kids' software might render him suitable for revamping the look of their newest product. He probably didn't need to list the reasons why Times New Roman was unsuitable, but the first was that it was ubiquitous, and the second was that it was boring. It had been designed in the early 1930s by Stanley Morison, a brilliant typographer whose influence on modern publishing was immense, to update *The Times* newspaper. This work had nothing in common

Microsoft Bob, a dog in
search of a font

with the way papers are updated today – redesigns intended primarily to increase the impression of youthfulness and upend a decline in circulation. Its prime intention was clarity; Morison maintained that 'a type which is to have anything like a present, let alone a future, will neither be very "different" nor very "jolly".'

But types have their time, and in the middle of the 1990s, at what was still the dawn of the digital age, Vincent Connare set about proving Morison wrong.

In many ways, Comic Sans existed before Connare made it legitimate by giving it a name. It existed, naturally enough, in comics and comic books (indeed the typeface was originally called Comic Book). One of the books that Connare had by his desk at Microsoft was *Batman: The Dark Knight Returns*, by Frank Miller with Klaus Janson and Lynn Varley. This

Watchmen – a dark inspiration for Comic Sans

told the tale of the elderly justice-doer jumping from his anxious retirement to take on terrible foes, only to find that he was even more unpopular with Gotham authorities than ever. The book was a huge crossover hit, reaching people who would previously have been embarrassed to carry what was then becoming an acceptable art form, the graphic novel. Along with Alan Moore's and Dave Gibbon's *Watchmen*, another influence on Connare, it marked the point where comics staked their claim as both literature and art.

Batman: The Dark Knight Returns was not that dissimilar from DC and Marvel comics of old, although it was now increasingly sinister, its characters taunted by terrible inner demons. Its value to the typographer was that it achieved that near-sublime melding of visuals and text, where one didn't swamp the other, and both could be absorbed simultaneously. It was like watching a perfectly subtitled film. When the Joker, seemingly dying, spits out 'I'LL ... SEE YOU ... IN HELL—' the reader skips from box to box gasping. This is perfect type, or at least perfect type suited to the medium; it might look odd in a Bible.

This was Connare's goal too, but he was aware that comic-book text was not always used so seamlessly. Those not exposed to comic books for years would perhaps be more familiar with Roy Lichtenstein's pop art type, inspired both by comics of the 1950s and the poetry of Phil Spector records. There was a primitive irony in Lichtenstein's use of the words 'WHAAM!' and 'AAARRRGGGHHH!!!', and a knowing humour in his yellow-haired damsels sobbing, 'That's the way it should have begun! But it's hopeless!' But this was obtrusive type, type with an arresting message.

Of course, Connare knew that both Lichtenstein and Frank Miller's Batman didn't use type at all, but letters that had been hand-drawn for each box. This gave it great flexibility and variety – no two letters exactly the same, the possibility of stressing a syllable by gently increasing the pressure on the nib – but Connare's appreciation of the craftsmanship did nothing to solve the problem of Microsoft Bob. This new software required a new type interface that looked as if it had been drawn by a creative and friendly hand (a hand that would hold your hand as you clicked through). His letters would be the same every time they were used but they would still look human.

Connare used the then-standard tool for designing type on a computer – Macromedia Fontographer – drawing each letter repeatedly within a grid until he got the style he required. He chose the equivalent of a child's blunted scissors – soft, rounded letters, with no sharp points to snag you. He drew both capitals and lower case, and printed them out to examine their dimensions when placed next to each

Aa Bb Cc Dd Ee Ff
Gg Hh Ii Jj Kk Ll Mm Nn
Oo Pp Qq Rr Ss Tt Uu
Vv Ww Xx Yy Zz

Comic Sans in all its childlike glory

other. Like most designers, he had a way of relaxing his eyes so that he could concentrate on the white paper behind the letters, gauging the space between the characters, the space between lines of text and their 'weight' – how light or bold they were, how much ink they used on a page, how many pixels they occupied on screen.

He then sent what he had made to the people working on Microsoft Bob, and they replied with bad news. Everything in the software package had been set with Times New Roman measurements – not only the choice and size of the type, but also the size of the speech bubbles that contained it. Comic Sans was slightly larger than Times New Roman, so it couldn't just be slotted in.

Microsoft Bob duly appeared in its formal state, and was not a success. No one officially blamed the unsuitable typeface. But not long afterwards, Connare's work was adopted for Microsoft Movie Maker, a distinct hit. And thus the typeface intended only as a solution to a problem took off.

Comic Sans went global after it was included as a supplementary typeface in Windows 95. Now everyone in the world could not only see it, but use it. Because it was irreverent and naive, it may have appeared better suited to the heading of your student essay than something with a heavier formality like Clarendon (which dates back to 1845). People also began to use it on restaurant menus, greeting cards and birthday invitations, and self-printed posters stapled to trees. It was viral advertising before such a thing existed, and like a good joke it was funny at first. Connare explained why it worked so well. 'Because it's sometimes better than Times New Roman, that's why.'

Then Comic Sans began to appear in other places: on the sides of ambulances, on online porn sites, on the backs of the shirts worn by the Portuguese national basketball team, on the BBC and in *Time* magazine, in adverts for Adidas boots. It became corporate, and suddenly Times New Roman didn't seem so bad any more.

In the new century, people began to get upset with Comic Sans, at first in a comic way, and then in a more emetic one. Bloggers turned against it, a dangerous thing, and Vincent Connare found himself at the centre of an Internet hate campaign. A husband and wife cottage industry sprang up

The bunny gets it – hard-hitting propaganda from the Ban Comic Sans website

around it, with Holly and David Combs offering mail-order 'Ban Comic Sans' mugs, caps and T-shirts. Alongside their own manifesto:

> We understand font selection is a matter of personal preference and that many people may disagree with us. We believe in the sanctity of typography and that the traditions and established standards of this craft should be upheld throughout all time ... Type's very qualities and characteristics communicate to readers a meaning beyond mere syntax.

The Combs, joint authors of a book called *Peel*, which documents the social history of the sticker, met one Saturday at a synagogue in Indianapolis; Holly says she was smitten as soon as they started discussing fonts. Both of them were clearly fans of type with authenticity and purpose, as their manifesto makes clear:

> When designing a 'Do Not Enter' sign, the use of a heavy-stroked, attention-commanding font such as **Impact** or **Arial Black** is appropriate. Typesetting such a message in Comic Sans would be ludicrous ... analogous to showing up for a black tie event in a clown costume.

The Combs' manifesto then began to sound like something the Futurists would write after too much absinthe, calling on the proletariat to rise up against the evil of Comic Sans, and to sign a petition for its prohibition.

Their website has attracted international feedback, highlighting the far-reaching and rapid spread of a font in the digital world. One post from South Africa lamented, 'I am forced to study a national language called Afrikaans, which is similar to Flemish. Almost every textbook is printed ENTIRELY in Comic Sans.'

The campaign also neatly demonstrated that the public, beyond the world of type design, has an awareness and an opinion about the everyday appearance of words. The *Wall Street Journal* wrote a column about Comic Sans and the banning movement on its front page (in its dour Dow Text font with a crisp Retina headline), explaining that the typeface was so unpopular that it was becoming retro chic, like lava lamps. *Design Week* went so far as to put Comic Sans on its cover, with a provocative Lichtenstein-style speech bubble asking, 'The world's favourite font!?'

The Combs don't really believe that Comic Sans is the plague of our time. In interviews they sound reasonable: 'Comic Sans looks great on a candy packet,' says Dave Combs. 'A place where it doesn't look great, in my opinion, is on a tombstone.' You've actually seen that? 'Yes, actually I have.' Where else was no good? 'I was in a doctor's office,' Holly Combs remembers, 'and there was a whole brochure describing irritable bowel syndrome ...'

Connare could have taken this one of two ways, but he was smart and appreciated the attention. He came to Comic Sans' defence, but also acknowledged its strict limitations. Like Dr Johnson's lexicographers, type designers can rarely expect acclaim, but they do well if they avoid recriminations.

And they rarely receive even ignominious fame, unlike Connare, who for a while became the most famous type designer in the world.

In the sixteen years after he developed Comic Sans, Connare has designed several other noteworthy typefaces, notably Trebuchet, which is a nicely rounded semi-formal humanist font ideal for web design.* But his fame rests with his original creation. 'Most everyday people that aren't in my industry know the font,' he says. I get introduced as the Comic Sans Guy. "What do you do?" they ask. "I design type." "What do you design?" "You might have heard of Comic Sans." And everybody says yes.'

One reason for this may be Comic Sans' emotional attributes, not least its warmth. Connare has written a monograph about his own type hero, William Addison Dwiggins, who in 1935 designed Electra, a sturdy book face that he intended to reflect the clanking machine age, its edges like the sparks and spits from a furnace. This too was emotional type, and Dwiggins envisaged a conversation in which he would justify his ambitions. 'If you don't get your type warm it will be no use at all for setting down *warm* human ideas – just a box full of rivets ... By jickity, I'd like to make a type that fitted 1935 all right enough, but I'd like to make it *warm* – so full of blood and personality that it would jump at you.' (Dwiggins was a man for the catchy phrase: he is credited with inventing the term 'graphic design'.)

* Both Trebuchet and Comic Sans are highly regarded by those who work with dyslexic children – their easy, unthreatening clarity proving far more accessible than harsher and more traditional fonts.

Connare can sometimes be elliptical about his fame. 'If you love Comic Sans, you don't know much about typography. If you hate it, you really don't know much about typography, either, and you should get another hobby.' And sometimes, rather than regale new acquaintances with the whole naive saga, he can email them a pdf slideshow. This shows not only odd uses of his font, but also a letter he received from the Ban Comic Sans campaigners thanking him for being 'a good sport'; on subsequent slides he showed a letter of appreciation from Disney after it used Comic Sans at its theme parks (it was signed by Mickey Mouse). His conclusion as to why Comic Sans has become one of the most widely used fonts in the world is arresting: people like it, he says, 'because it's not like a typeface'.

By jickity indeed. This suggests that, even in the digital age, we don't know very much about type, and may in fact be frightened of it. Here is something that has always been central to our lives, but when the pull-down menu offers us the opportunity to choose type for our own ends we appear to opt for the one that most reminds us of the schoolroom. At every opportunity our computer asks whether we might like to spend the day with Baskerville, Calibri, Century, Georgia, Gill Sans, Lucida, Palatino or Tahoma. But we choose old Comic Sans.

Perhaps this is just as it should be. In its attempt to resemble handwriting, Comic Sans has its roots in type from the Middle Ages. It is the logical conclusion to a technological breakthrough that transformed everything. Of course, if Johannes Gutenberg had imagined that his greatest endeavour would end up as a funny sign above a funeral parlour he might just have wrapped his plump stained fingers around all the printer's ink in Europe and thrown it in the sea.

But come on Johannes, loosen up! Tell us a joke! As the *Wall Street Journal* observed, at least Comic Sans has stepped out from under a computer's toolbar to become a punchline:

> Comic Sans walks into a bar and the bartender says, 'We don't serve your type.'

2

CAPITAL OFFENCE

On 25th September 2007, a woman named Vicki Walker committed a type crime so calamitous that it cost her not only her job, but almost her sanity. Walker was working as an accountant in a New Zealand health agency, and there was an email to send. Regrettably, she ignored the only rule that everyone who has ever emailed knows: CAPITAL LETTERS LOOK LIKE YOU HATE SOMEONE AND ARE SHOUTING.

It was a Tuesday afternoon. Walker pressed 'Send' on this instruction:

TO ENSURE YOUR STAFF CLAIM IS PROCESSED AND PAID, PLEASE DO FOLLOW THE BELOW CHECKLIST.

Not the written word's finest hour in lots of ways, but hardly a sackable offence. The letters were in blue, and elsewhere her email contained bold black and red. She worked for ProCare in Auckland, a company which clearly placed great pride in knowing when and when not to hold down the Caps button, though it did not have an email etiquette guide at the time Vicki Walker splurged on upper case.

Upper and lower case? The term comes from the position of the loose metal or wooden letters laid in front of the traditional compositor's hands before they were used to form a word – the commonly used ones on an accessible lower level, the capitals above them, waiting their turn. Even with this distinction, the compositor would still have to 'mind their ps and qs', so alike were they when each letter was dismantled from a block of type and then tossed back into the compartments of a tray.

The correct use of type varies over time. These days, corporate edicts are common, and memos come down from on high like tablets of stone: thou shalt use only Arial on both internal and external communications. But who is to say that lower-case Arial from 1982 is preferable to the way we communicated in TRAJAN CAPITALS on the pediments of public buildings in ancient Rome? And how did our eyes switch from accepting one over the other, to the point where a thoughtless choice of capitals-all-the-way became a cause of headaches and dismissals?

The upper and lower case

Vicki Walker was sacked three months after her email was deemed to have caused 'disharmony in the workplace', which would have been laughable had it not caused her so much distress. Twenty months later, after re-mortgaging her house and borrowing money from her sister to fight her case, Walker appealed successfully for unfair dismissal, and was awarded $17,000.

There have always been rules of type, and type etiquette. Say you are designing a jacket for a new edition of Jane Austen's *Pride and Prejudice*. The book is out of copyright and so has cost you nothing, the beautiful jacket illustration of a secret garden has been done by a friend, and now all you have to do is find a suitable typeface for the title and author, and then the text inside. For the jacket type, conventional wisdom would be to choose something like Didot, which first appeared at around the time Austen was writing and looks very classy with its extreme range of fine and stronger lines, especially in italics (*Pride and Prejudice*). This font will fit right in, and will sell books to people who like classic editions. But if you wanted to reach a different market, the sort who might read Kate Atkinson or Sebastian Faulks, you may opt for something less fusty, perhaps Ambroise Light, which, like Didot, has a stylish French pedigree.

For the text of the book, you might consider a digital update of Bembo – perhaps **Bembo Book**? Originally cut from metal in the 1490s, this classic roman typeface retains a consistent readability. And it fits the overriding principle that typefaces should mostly pass unrecognized in daily life; that they should inform but not alarm. A font on a book jacket should merely pull you in; once it has created the desired atmosphere it does well to slink away, like the host at a party.

There are exceptions, of course, and a brilliant one is John Gray's bestseller, *Men Are From Mars, Women Are From Venus*, in which the designer Andrew Newman chose Arquitectura for the male lines and Centaur for the female ones. Arquitectura looks manly because it is tall, solid, slightly space-age, rooted and implacable. Centaur, despite its bullish name, looks like it has been written by hand, has thin and thick strokes, and is charming and elegant (obviously this is gross sexual stereotyping, but *Men Are From Mars, Women Are From Venus* is pop-psychology).

Fonts have sexual stereotypes, too

This then is another rule: type can have gender. The understanding is that heavy bold jagged fonts are mostly male (try **Colossalis**), and whimsical, lighter curly fonts are mostly female (perhaps *ITC Brioso Pro Italic Display* from the Adobe Wedding Collection). You can subvert this form, but never the automatic associations that type infers. It's the same with colour: you see a baby dressed in pink – that's a girl. Type has us conditioned from birth, and it has taken more than five hundred years to begin to shake it free.

Johannes Gutenberg didn't pay much regard to the gender of type when he made his first letters in the 1440s. And he didn't much care about finding a suitable font for each new project, or even changing the course of Western history. What he cared about was making money.

Gutenberg was born in Mainz, near Frankfurt, the son of a wealthy merchant with links to the local mint. His family moved to Strasbourg when Gutenberg was young, but the details of his early working life are cloudy. There are records of his involvement with gems, metalwork and mirrors, but by the late 1440s he was known to be back in Mainz borrowing money to make ink and printing equipment.

Gutenberg's vision concerned automation, consistency and recycling. He is unlikely to have known of the far earlier printing methods in China and Korea, most of which involved the one-off production of books with woodblocks and cast bronze type. Certainly he was the first to have mastered the principles of mass production in Europe, and his innovations with casting reusable letters set the pattern for printing for the next five hundred years. The book became cheaper and more available, and what was once the sole province of the church and the wealthy became in time a source of pleasure and enlightenment for all educated classes. What a dangerous tool he unleashed.

How was this achieved? With dexterity, patience and some ingenuity. Gutenberg's experience of smithery had taught him the principles of hard and soft metals, and of hammering hallmarks and other symbols into silver and gold. He was equally familiar with liquid alloys, and at some point in the late 1440s it is likely that an idea forged in his mind: what if all these combined techniques could be applied to printing?

Early printers at work in this engraving from 1568. Cast type is being arranged by compositors in the background.

All the books Gutenberg had seen up to this point would have been handwritten. To modern eyes, their script can often look almost mechanical, though this was a result of painstaking work by a professional scribe hunched for months over a single volume. Complete words could be engraved into individual blocks of metal or wood and then inked, but this would take even longer to create a book. But what if it were possible to transform this process by casting an alphabet in small pieces of movable type that could be reused and reconfigured as often as each new page of a document or book required?

Gutenberg's precise method of typefounding is unknown, but popular wisdom suggests that it was at least similar to the first documented process two decades later (and the method that dominated printing up until 1900). This begins with punchcutting – carving a letter in reverse on the end of a steel rod a few inches long. The punch is then hammered into softer metal, often copper, forming an indented 'matrix' to be fitted into a hand-held wooden mould with the aid of a spring. Hot metal – a mixture of lead, tin and antimony – is poured into the mould with a ladle, and hardens swiftly into a single letter at the tip of a slither of type, ready to be aligned into words. Taken as a whole, a font is born, although the process of spacing, moulding and finishing is a lot more skilled than suggested here. The single regular alphabet would be augmented by many duplicate letters, as well as punctuation and spaces; it is believed that Gutenberg cast almost three hundred different letterforms for his two-volume 1,282-page Bible of 1454–55.

Once the font was ready, a page would be carefully assembled (in its mirror image), and tightened in a wooden frame or 'chase', and once enough copies had been printed, the block was broken up and the type used again. The printing made the process swift, while the type made it economical; thus did we witness the birth of mass production.

The scale of Gutenberg's achievements is inestimable. He advanced not only the printing press but also new oil-based inks (thinner water-based inks failed to adhere to metal) in addition to what may be considered to be the first example of book marketing. He employed twenty assistants, some of them in a sales capacity; in an early version of the Frankfurt Book Fair in 1454, all 180 printed copies of his Bible were sold ahead of publication.

Gutenberg's role in the dissemination of debate, science and dissent – printing as the dual mouthpiece of human sense and human folly – was already being felt by the time of his death in 1468. (He did not die wealthy, having surrendered his printing equipment after an unsuccessful legal battle with his principal

The world's first font – Gutenberg's Textura

benefactor Johannes Fust.) But his role in the cutting of type is less clear, and certainly another name deserves equal recognition. Peter Schoeffer, who joined Gutenberg in Mainz after studying calligraphy at the Sorbonne, is believed to have had a significant role in the earliest experiments in punchcutting, though his contribution is largely forgotten.

Gutenberg's and Schoeffer's first texts resembled – in fact imitated – handwritten scripts, in part because this was what people were used to, and in part because he believed it would be the only way for his books to achieve the same market price as the ones they were replacing. The type used for their famous Bible has come to be known as Textura – taking its name from one of the 'writing hands' of the time, part of a group known as Schwabacher (blackletter) script favoured by monkish scribes. But for other work, including the Mainz Indulgences (church documents purchased by a 'sinner' marking a suitable period of penance), their type had a more open and human feel which has become known as Bastarda.

At the British Library in London, a copy of Gutenberg's Bible lies under thick glass in a dimly lit room on the first floor, where it shares hushed space with other treasures, including the Magna Carta, the Lindisfarne Gospels and the Sherborne Missal, as well as Captain Scott's diary, a manuscript by Harold Pinter and handwritten lyrics by the Beatles. The Bible is printed on paper (the Library has another printed on vellum) and has a provenance shrouded in intrigue and crossings out on title pages. It is one of just forty-eight known surviving copies (most of these are incomplete – only twelve intact paper copies and four complete vellum copies exist), and each has variations in text, lineage, spacing and illumination. Spectroscopy has revealed the exact pigments used in the illuminated capitals and opening lines, a combination of lead tin yellow, vermillion, verdigris, chalk, gypsum, lead white and carbon black.

These days, digitization enables us to view the copies online without the need for a trip to the Euston Road, although to do so would be to deny oneself one of the great pleasures in life. The first book ever printed in Europe – heavy, luxurious, pungent and creaky – does not read particularly well on an iPhone.

Fonts were once known as founts. Fonts and founts weren't the same as typefaces, and typefaces weren't the same as type. In Europe the transition from fount to font was essentially complete by the 1970s, a grudging acceptance of the Americanization of the word. The two were used interchangeably as early as the 1920s, although some whiskered English traditionalists will still insist on 'fount' in an elitist way, in the hope that it will stretch their authenticity all the way back to Caxton, the great British printer of Chaucer. But most people have stopped caring. There are more important things to worry about, such as what the word actually means.

In the days when type was set by hand, a font was a complete set of letters of a typeface in one particular size and style – every different a, b and c in upper and lower case, each pound or dollar sign and punctuation mark. There would be many duplicates, the exact amount dependent on their common usage, but always more Es than Js. The word is derived from 'fund', the fund (amount) of type from which the letters are selected. These days a font refers simply to a particular typeface, which may have ten or twenty fonts, each weight and style on the page a little different. But in common parlance we use font and typeface interchangeably, and there are worse sins.

Definitions should not cloud our appreciation of type, but some classifications can be useful in understanding the subject's history and usage. Just as it is entirely possible to have a pleasant afternoon in a gallery with no knowledge of art theory or an artist's place in the firmament, one can wander around the streets admiring typefaces on signs and shops with not a care for their history. But it may increase our love of them if we know who made them, and what they were aiming for. And for this we need to define a few words in the typographic language.

In 1977, the *Guardian* ran an elaborate and now famous April Fools' Day hoax marking the tenth anniversary of the independence of San Serriffe: a republic whose every name was taken from the world of fonts. Floating freely in the Indian Ocean, the state had undergone a period of rapid prosperity (due in no small part to its phosphate reserves), and the seven-page supplement was full of intriguing information about the benign union-busting activities of General Che Pica and the port of Clarendon, and the Caslon-speaking, theatre-going activities of the native Flongs.

The hoax was a cross between Woody Allen's *Bananas* and the BBC radio game 'Mornington Crescent' – a parallel world where only the most steel-hearted would litter its

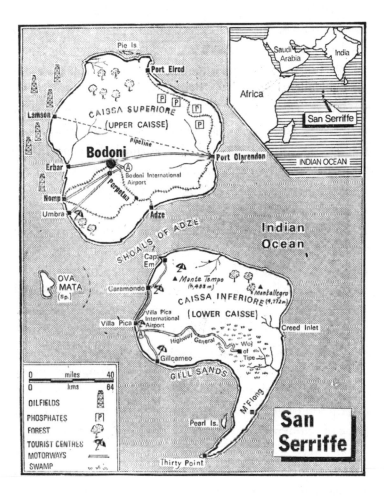

San Serriffe's archipelago: the islands of Upper and Lower Caisse. Note the enticing beach of Gill Sands in the sweep of the lower isle.

beaches (Gill Sands) with cynicism. Some readers, it is said, tried to book a holiday there, though travel agents were unable to locate Bodoni International Airport, the quaint inlet of Garamondo or the vaste swathe of uninhabitable Perpetua. They even had trouble locating the islands themselves, both the round Caissa Superiore and the curlier Caissa Inferiore, which together formed the shape of a semi-colon. San Serriffe drifted into legend, and it may have caused those readers unfamiliar with type lore to dig out the dictionary.

Bodoni and Baskerville are both serif fonts, while Gill Sans is a sans serif. The difference lies at the feet or tips of the letters, with a serif typeface carrying a finishing stroke often appearing to ground the letter on the page. This could be the base of an E, M, N or P, but it could also be the left-upper flick of an r or the roof of a k. It makes the letters look traditional, square, honest and carved – and their lineage can be traced back as far as the Roman emperor Trajan, whose Column in Rome, completed in 113, bears an inscription in his honour and serves as the most influential piece of anonymous stone carving in 2,000 years.

Sans serif faces may appear less formal and more contemporary, but they can be as redolent of tradition as a brass band. Many have a very classical and Roman form – indeed sans serif lettering existed in the Ancient World –

inui

It's all in the feet and tips: remove those dark areas (the serifs) and you get a sans serif

Trajan's Column – the classic (serif) font of the classical world

and when they appeared on buildings in fascist Italy between the wars they fitted right in, as if they had been there for centuries. They are durable and may be monumental, and while Futura, Helvetica and Gill Sans are the best known, there are countless numbers in our daily lives. The oldest sans serif type is probably **CASLON EGYPTIAN** from 1816 and through the nineteenth century they became popular mainly as display fonts, for use on posters.

However, in the following century sans serif type took on a very different character, as a new generation of designers fused the Roman and display traditions with modern style. Nothing looked so good stuck on the side of a new machine, or, as with Edward Johnston's typeface, on the London Underground. The roots of this new sans serif lay in Germany, in a font known as Akzidenz Grotesk, released in

1898. But it was given a new life in Britain by Johnston and by Eric Gill's Gill Sans, and by others in Germany, Holland and – most notably – in post-war Switzerland, where Univers and Helvetica arose to spearhead modernism's spread across the world. So we'd best think of the type now as European.

Because there are so many typefaces, there have been many attempts to classify them into definable groups. But type is a living element, and it will resist absolute categorization until it is worn thin; a good single letter in a vivid typeface has enough energy in itself to leap free from any box. Still, a few loose categories can at least make visible the host of variations in type, and help us cope with the possibility of explaining a font to someone who can't see it (which, before email attachments, was a real bonus).

The key system of type classifications is called Vox, after its French originator, Maximilien Vox. It appeared in the 1950s and was the basis for the 1967 British Standards Classification of Typefaces. This delineated nine basic forms, from *Humanist*, *Didone* and *Slab-serif* to *Lineale* and *Graphic* (Lineale was another word for sans serif). It tried to be strict in its definitions, but often reverted to vagueness: 'The R usually has a curved leg,' it observed of the *Grotesques*. 'The ends of the curved strokes are usually oblique,' it said of the *Neo-grotesques*.

More recently, the big suppliers of digital type, such as Adobe and ITC, have attempted their own systems of clarification. This is intended to help with searches and sales at their online sites, but generally shows the near imposs-ibility (and perhaps futility) of accurate categorization.

shady
flax ↕

Lesson one in the anatomy of type: ascenders and descenders (top), ligature and x-height.

Within each typeface, a single letter has its own geography. This requires an exact language that is charming and unforgiving, jargon which began with the punchcutter from the fifteenth century and has resisted all attempts at digital corruption. We have already encountered some of these – *counters* being the enclosed or semi-enclosed areas of a letter, within an o, b or n, for example; while the *bowl* is the curved shape of the g, b, etc; and *stems* are the main constructional elements – which may be thick or thin depending on design.

A *bracketed serif* has a curved element like a tree trunk, an *unbracketed* one is a straight line, while a *wedge serif* falls at a geometric angle. The *x-height* of a letter is the distance between the *base line* (the line in an exercise book) and the *mean line* (the top of a lower-case letter); an *ascender* rises above the mean line, a *descender* below the base line.

Some type vocabulary has an internal beauty of its own (or it did when all type was metal). Much of this is anthropomorphic, treating letters as living life-forms: the whole character is known as the *body*, the blank space below the raised letter is the *beard*, the flat side of the metal type is the *shoulder*, while the whole raised letterform is the *face*. At the San Serriffe hospital you could have a ligature, and the result would often be grotesque. Traditionally, a *ligature* has meant a light linking flourish between two letters that are joined together (such as fl or ae, which require less white

A depth scale – once a key part of a typographer's toolkit

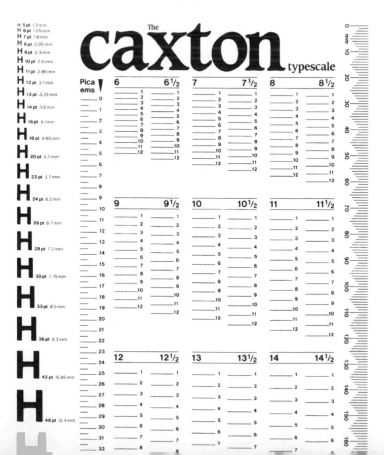

space between them than if the letters were used on their own). These days, commonly, a ligature (a feature of both serif and sans serif faces) refers to the two letters themselves, used as if they were one.

A *grotesque face* is not necessarily an ugly one; a *grot* is a name applied to a certain type of sans serif type, usually from the nineteenth century, with some variation in the thickness of letter strokes. A *neo-grotesque* is more uniform, has less of a square look to the curved letters, and works very well in lower case in small point sizes.

And then there is maths. The *point size* can be used both as a unit of measuring type and the space between it. For regular newspaper and book text, 8pt to 12pt usually satisfies. There are 72pts to an inch. 1pt is 0.013833 inches. Typographers group them in *picas*: 12pts to a pica and 6 picas to an inch. There have been many historical and national variations, and metal and digital measures differ slightly, but today we almost have an international standard: in the US, 1pt = 0.351mm; in Europe 1pt = 0.376mm.

But the maths, geography and vocabulary of type should never obscure the most basic fact of all: regular or italics, light or bold, upper or lower case – the fonts that work best are the ones that allow us to read without ruining our eyes.

Gill Sans

Eric Gill is remembered for many things: his engravings in wood and stone, his lifelong passion for lettering, his devotion to English craftsmanship – and his typefaces, notably Gill Sans, one of the twentieth century's earliest and classic sans serif fonts.

And then there is that other thing: Gill's scandalous and ceaseless sexual experimentation. In 1989, Fiona MacCarthy published a biography of the artist that featured stomach-curdling detail of his dramatically outré meanderings with his daughters, sister and dog, as recorded in his own diaries. The photographs of Gill in his full-length smock were unsettling enough, but then came the descriptions of his incestuous and canine arousals ('Continued experiment with dog … and discovered that a dog will join with a man').

MacCarthy argues that Eric Gill's priapism was as much a product of an inquisitive mind as his exquisite craftsmanship, that 'the urge to try things out, to push experience to limits was part of his nature and part of his importance as a social and religious commentator and an artist'. Possibly true, although some still shudder with revulsion at the mention of his name – a recent online forum at Typophile debating a boycott of Gill Sans on account of its creator's past. Most have taken a more bemused view. Indeed, the American designer Barry Deck, who achieved fame for Template Gothic, a fancifully fluid sans font, in 1990, designed a loose tribute to Gill called Canicopulus.

Oddly enough, Gill Sans is itself a curiously sexless font. It began to take shape when Gill was living in the Welsh mountains in the mid-1920s. Here he tried out sans serif forms in his notebooks and on signs to guide tourists around the monastery in Capel-y-ffin. In his autobiography, Gill explained that sans serif was the obvious choice when 'a forward-minded bookseller of Bristol asked me to paint his shop fascia'. The long wooden sign in question, for Douglas Cleverdon, led to something else – for after seeing a sketch of these letters, Gill's old friend Stanley Morison commissioned him to design an original sans face for Monotype.

Its impact was instant and is still reverberating. Gill Sans appeared in 1928, when its creator was forty-four. It was the most British of types, not only in its appearance (spare, proper

Gill Sans begins to take shape on a Bristol shopfront

and reservedly proud), but also in its usage – adopted by the Church of England, the BBC, the first Penguin book jackets and British Railways (where it was used on everything from timetables to restaurant menus). Each showed Gill Sans to be a supremely workable text face, carefully structured for mass reproduction. It wasn't the most charming or radiant, and not perhaps the most endearing choice for literary fiction, but it was ideal for catalogues and academia. It was an inherently trustworthy font, never fussy, consistently practical.

Despite his big hit, Gill never thought much of himself as a typeface man. His gravestone, which implores the visitor to 'Pray For Me', casts him merely as a stone carver, one of the rarest representations of modesty in the world of graphic design. In fact, Gill designed twelve other typefaces, including the popular classical serifs Perpetua and Joanna, as well as Felicity, Solus, Golden Cockerel, Aries, Jubilee and Bunyan.

Joanna was named after his youngest daughter, with whom, MacCarthy suggests, he had less of a dubious relationship than with his other two. He used it beautifully to set his *Essay on Typography*, which was really a treatise on the effects of mechanization on the purity of the soul. It reveals a demonstratively

The first Penguin book, printed in 1935, with title and author set in quintessentially British Gill Sans. The Penguin logo here is Bodoni Ultra Bold but was itself later changed to Gill Sans.

exact character ('The title page should be set in the same style of type as the book and preferably in the same size'), and his pronouncements elsewhere suggest a wholly unromantic one. 'The shapes of letters do not derive their beauty from any sensual or sentimental reminiscences,' he wrote. 'No one can say that the O's roundness appeals to us only because it is like that of an apple or of a girl's breast or of the full moon. Letters are things, not pictures of things.'

Eric Gill in his smock, *c.* 1908

Gill died in 1940, just as his most famous font began appearing on the Ministry of Information's wartime warnings about blackouts, careless talk and the recruitment of the Home Guard.

3

Legibility vs Readability

In a wood, somewhere in England, rifles in hand, you have been watching

    Arthur Lowe (proud, pompous walk)

    John Le Mesurier (leafy camouflaged helmet, looking nervous)

    Clive Dunn (brave gaze, cold steel)

    John Laurie (anxious, doomed)

    James Beck (crafty draw on cheeky fag)

    Arnold Ridley (may need to be excused)

    Ian Lavender (blue scarf, mum's insistence)

This is the closing sequence to *Dad's Army*, Britain's much-loved TV comedy about the Second World War, produced in the late 1960s/early 1970s and repeated ever since. The actors' credits are in **Cooper Black**, which sells not only things we now consider to be retro and classic, such as **Kickers** or **Spacehoppers**, but also anything intended to be warm, fuzzy, homely, reliable and reassuring, like **easyJet**.

The lettering on the side of planes had rarely implied fun ('we're one of you! climb aboard!') before easyJet tried it, and so strong is this typographic branding that no one has successfully imitated it. (Although the budget airline's chief rival, Ryanair, once used **Arial Extra Bold** – attracted perhaps by its name – before moving to a proprietary font.)

EasyJet's branding soon extended to the easyGroup's other products, and was discussed in the company's mission statement:

> Our visual identity, known as the 'Getup', is an essential part of the easyJet Brand Licence and is cast in stone! It is defined as: a) white lettering on an orange background (Pantone 021c on glossy print materials; on other surfaces the nearest practicable equivalent), and b) in Cooper Black font (not bold, italics, outline nor underlined), the word 'easy' in lower case, followed (without space) by another word ...

Cooper Black was a good find. It is rare for a new company to select a pre-digital unmodernized classic face from the shelf and not revive or tweak it in some way, but here was an exception. Like so many fonts that have stuck, it was designed in the 1920s, and became instantly popular. Oswald Bruce Cooper, a former Chicago advertising man, was commissioned by the foundry Barnhart Brothers & Spindler to make something that they could sell to advertisers (and something that looked suspiciously similar to Pabst Extra Bold, designed several years before by Frederic W Goudy for the American brewing firm).

Its success soon allayed Cooper's fear that he would only achieve 'a tiresome effect from the too frequent repetition of the same quirk and curve'. In fact he achieved something spectacular – a serif face that looked like a sans serif. Cooper Black is the sort of font the oils in a lava lamp would form if smashed to the floor. Its creator believed it ideal 'for far-sighted printers with near-sighted customers'. There are little nicks at the tops and bases of letters, and they give the font a solid flat weight on a page; without them, the type would always have been appearing to roll away. For a font with such a thickset look, it retains a remarkably unthreatening demeanour. Partly this is due to its stout and pudgy descenders, its large lower-case letters in relation to its capitals, and the limited white peering through the counters of the a, b, d, e and g. It is usually employed quite bunched up, for excessive spacing between letters would make it break up very fast, confusing the eye.*

Cooper Black looks best from afar, as easyJet recognized. Before then, its most famous appearance was probably on the classic Beach Boys album *Pet Sounds*. Like many record covers of the time, this printed each song title on the front

---

* The ultimate Cooper Black font, the connoisseur's choice, is ATF Cooper Hilite, a wet-look 3-D type, created by adding an internal white line. This is the equivalent of go-faster stripes on the side of a car, giving each letter the pumped-up steroid appearance of an inner tube fit to burst.

Cooper Black counters strut their stuff
(the d and g are Cooper Hilite)

of the sleeve – above the photograph of the band feeding goats at the zoo. Cooper Black for the band name and title is iconic, not least because the letters are touching, and reflect Robert Indiana's then very much in-vogue 'Love' logo. But its weakness as a text font is immediately clear. '**Wouldn't It Be Nice/You Still Believe In Me**,' the first line runs, before our brain unscrambles the rest of the offering, '**God Only Knows**', '**Sloop John B**' and the others. The 12-inch record sleeve gets away with it; the CD cover is very hard work.

The graphics people responsible for the *Dad's Army* credits knew they'd have problems once the big stars with the big lettering left our screens; the show's lesser characters are credited for a briefer period, and with no pictures: 'Featuring Philip Madoc as the U-Boat Captain … with Bill Pertwee as Chief Warden Hodges …' Before 42-inch widescreens, viewers couldn't possibly handle all of this in small Cooper Black, so only the actors' names appear in this font, and the parts they're playing are in something resembling Helvetica.

This is one difference between legibility and readability: at small sizes, **Cooper Black is legible but not very readable**. But some type is meant to be seen rather than read (a type

Cooper Black – looks great from afar, and the bigger the better

designer once compared this attribute to a dress designed to look great on the catwalk but provide no protection against the elements). Font-as-couture is a common analogy. Adrian Frutiger, designer of one of the most popular modern fonts, Univers, had another: 'The work of a type designer is just like that of a dressmaker,' he noted. 'Clothing the constant, human form.' Or as the book designer Alan Fletcher put it, 'a typeface is an alphabet in a straitjacket'.

As with fashion, the design of type is an alarmingly vibrant art form. It refuses ossification. Like the wildest genres of modern art, it is the newest things that upset the traditionalists (although they will seldom admit this, criticizing instead its manners or its lack of proper schooling). The traditionalist will argue that no one buys a typeface to hang on the wall, while the more traditional still may argue that only when a typeface is beautiful enough to be displayed in a gallery may it also be considered suitable for print.

But beauty demands discipline. It is possible that the amateur creatively unleashed by the computer may produce something beautiful, but will it work on the page as practical type? Will all the letters look equally good next to any other letter, or will the spacing between them create textual migraine? (The science of proportional spacing between pairs of letters is known as kerning – ensuring, for example, that slanting letters such as A or V nudge up to adjacent letters, consistently more pleasing to the eye; the 'kern' is that part of a character that overhangs or underhangs its body and invades the space of the letter next to it.)

Tastes change, thank heavens. A typeface that would once have been regarded as too tight, its letters nuzzling each other and its words colliding, may now, through the power of advertising and familiarity, appear the height of modernity and legibility. It may hold this exalted position for a decade or so, before something dangerously over-spaced renders it passé. A sign or a slogan set entirely in lower case (perhaps McDonald's **i'm lovin' it**) was once considered blasphemous; now it is merely dull. And the old principle of legibility, once the prime factor in any consideration of good type, and defined with terrible severity by the French ophthalmologist Dr Louis Emile Javal at the beginning of the last century (and then slavishly followed by many designers), seems very outdated; our eyes and brains appreciate far more than the first scientists of type thought possible.

One of Dr Javal's theories now seems particularly absurd – that the most legible type is also the most beautiful.

In the 1940s, the most popular test of a font's legibility was the 'blink test'. Blinking relieves tired eyes in the same way as putting down heavy shopping relieves pressure on our palms; our eyes blink more when tired or under strain, and a familiar typeface will cause less fatigue. Under laboratory conditions – where light and type size are regulated, and the 'patient' (reader) is presented with the same text in many faces (the optician's sight chart yielding to the pursuit of both art and universal clarity) – the number of involuntary blinks was monitored on a handheld clicker.

According to a series of lectures given by John Biggs at the London College of Printing, the types that fared best in the blink tests were those that had survived for centuries and were always being revived and slightly modified: Bembo,

Bodoni, Garamond. It might have been easier to ask the patient which text they comprehended better, or which gave them less eyestrain, but such methods would have been subjective and unscientific.

Fortunately we also have more recent investigations. Many of these occurred in the 1970s at the Royal College of Art's Readability of Print Research Unit (in the computer age it became the slightly less ungainly Graphic Information Research Unit). Among its conclusions: people found type with strong distinctive strokes easier to read than flattened styles; and a greater distinction between letters led to a clearer (and faster) digest of information. The research confirmed that the key areas that make a letter most distinctive are its top half and right side, the eye using these flagposts to confirm what it anticipates may be there.

Other surveys suggested that most readers prefer bold faces over regular ones, although their legibility is about the same. Serif and sans serif faces are also equally legible, so long as the serifs aren't too heavy and thick. Typefaces

Bembo
Bodoni
Garamond

The old faithfuls – scientifically proven in the 1940s

with larger counters – the very opposite of Cooper Black – are also regarded as more legible, especially at smaller sizes where these counters could fill with ink.

Legibility is also defined by a less formal characteristic: taste. This is not the same as trendiness; rather it is popularity demonstrated by mass consumption. We like to think of our cultural tastes improving and maturing with age, but in the case of type design something else also happens: we are simply worn down by over-exposure.

The radical Californian type designer Zuzana Licko has a popular theory that 'you read best what you read most'. Heavy blackletter type was once considered more readable than a softer, less formal script, but merely through ubiquity. 'You need to use something that is not necessarily intrinsically more legible, but that people are used to seeing,' Licko observes, echoing the 1940s conclusions. 'Preferences for typefaces such as Times Roman exist by habit, because those typefaces have been around longest. When those typefaces

first came out, they were not what people were used to either. But because they got used, they have become extremely legible.'

Eric Gill had been of much the same mind ('Legibility, in practice, amounts simply to what one is accustomed to'). But the fact that this theory has gained Licko's

Zuzana Licko and Rudy VanderLans

imprimatur is significant, as she and her partner Rudy VanderLans are among the most respected contemporary type designers in the United States. The duo published a magazine, *Emigre*, which inspired a whole generation of graphic design students. Licko believes that when designing a typeface one must – as Matthew Carter put it – find 'the fascination greater than the frustration'. At the beginning, she says, as a typeface is conceptualized, 'every detail gets questioned. This process is fascinating because it makes you realize how each detail affects the resulting work, as many details are repeated among characters, which multiplies the effect. Eventually this can turn to frustration because it seems the process will never end ...'

An email conversation with Licko will elicit responses such as the one above, but the big question she won't help you with is why there are relatively few women type designers. 'Sorry,' she typed. 'I have no idea.'

Licko and her designer friends acknowledge that readability of any text font is best conferred by a number of features, ideally occurring concurrently (if these appear obvious, it is only because we take them for granted). Every letter of the alphabet must be distinct from each other to avoid confusion. The effect of letters on a reader should best be judged in context – as sentences and paragraphs – as it is only the overall shape of combined letters that may be judged either readable or not.

Such readability will be aided by regular paragraphs and sufficient margins, and by an acceptable line length (this is naturally dependent on the size of the text, but is ideally considered to be between ten and twelve words). The space between letters and their relationship to each other is as important as the space between lines (leading or pointing). There should be a contrast between thick and thin strokes, and letters should be in a regular proportion to each other. Variety in width is particularly important, with the upper half of letters being more readable than the lower half. The weight of letters in a block of text should generally be medium – too light a type will cause letters to appear grey and indistinct, while too dark will cause the letters to appear overly thick, wrecking distinguishing details and blocking out the background.

The simplicity of these observations is not reflected in the simplicity of their execution. Still harder to grasp is the realization that confronts every novice when designing a text font for the first time: despite all appearances, letters that appear to be of equal height may in fact be subtly different.

Reading a book or computer screen about a foot away from the eye, this is a difficult element to perceive, but

It is the reader's familiarity that accounts for legibility; it is the reader's fa with typefaces tha IT IS THE READER'S FAM WITH TYPEFACES THAT

'Totally Gothic' by Zuzana Licko shown in the 1996 Emigre fonts catalogue

it it it it

Left to right, Baskerville, Goudy Old Style, Sabon and Times New Roman undergo the stem test and dot test

when letters are enlarged to a couple of inches or more and set upon parallel lines, the slightly longer depth of round letters such as O, S and B becomes more apparent. Our brain demands evenness and certainty, but our eyes play tricks on us. If all letters were exactly the same height they wouldn't appear so: round and pointed letters would appear shorter.

It's an interesting party game: the dot of a dotted i in a traditional serif font is usually not directly over the top of the stem but slightly to the left. And the stem of a lower-case t will be slightly thicker at the base to avoid the appearance of frailty and the risk of toppling over backwards. In type, the appearance of beauty and elegance depends on trickery and skill – perhaps the most fruitful and longest-lasting collision of science and art.

The single most famous pronouncement on type was written in 1932 by a woman called Beatrice Warde, a friend (and sometime lover) of Eric Gill who was the face and voice of the Monotype Corporation in the 1920s and 30s.

There is a revealing photograph of Warde taken during a party in 1923. She is surrounded by more than thirty type men in sombre suits, all looking rather proud of themselves, and justly so: they ran the cream of American type foundries and were jointly responsible for the look of American letters. But none look quite as confident as Warde, the one person in a dress, sitting with a wry smile and her hands in her lap, fairly sure that she was actually in charge. In her early twenties, she was already an extremely busy woman, not only writing extensively about type in the leading graphic design journal *The Fleuron*, but also producing challenging manifestos (originally under the pseudonym Paul Beaujon, out of concern that the typographic community would pay little attention to a woman).

On 7th October 1930, Beatrice Warde addressed the British Typographers Guild at the St Bride Institute, just behind Fleet Street in London. Warde was an American, and her skill was communication. She found the perfect job as publicity manager for the Monotype Corporation in Surrey, one of the leading companies that produced typesetting machinery and typefaces. Her greatest feat may have been inspirational, lifting the spirits of her customers – printers and designers – by emphasizing the grandeur and responsibilities of their calling. 'What I'm really good at,' she reckoned, not long before she died in 1969, 'is standing up in front of an audience with no preparation at all, then for 50 minutes refusing to let them even wriggle an ankle.'

Why was she so strict? Because she had an unwavering belief in her own teaching, which itself displayed an element of the straitjacket. Despite her boasts, her talk to the British typographers had clearly undergone a lot of preparation, not least in its title, 'The Crystal Goblet, or Printing Should Be Invisible'.

THIS IS A
PRINTING-OFFICE

CROSS-ROADS OF CIVILIZATION

REFUGE OF ALL THE ARTS
AGAINST THE RAVAGES OF TIME

ARMOURY OF FEARLESS TRUTH
AGAINST WHISPERING RUMOUR

INCESSANT TRUMPET OF TRADE

FROM THIS PLACE **WORDS** MAY FLY ABROAD

NOT TO PERISH AS WAVES OF SOUND BUT FIXED IN TIME

NOT CORRUPTED BY THE HURRYING HAND BUT VERIFIED IN PROOF

FRIEND, YOU STAND ON SACRED GROUND:

THIS IS A PRINTING-OFFICE

Strong words from a strong-minded woman (in Albertus). Just about every printer in the country had a copy of Warde's broadside on display.

Her simple and sound theory was that the best type existed merely to communicate an idea. It was not there to be noticed, much less admired. The more a reader becomes aware of a typeface or a layout on a page, the worse that typography is. Her wine analogy was cool and mature, and perhaps now appears a little trite: the clearer the glass, the more its contents could be appreciated; not for her the lavish opaque golden goblet symbolized by old gothic script where the heavily barred E resembles a portcullis.

She also made a fine point distinguishing legibility from readability. A type in a larger size is not necessarily more readable, although taken by itself in an optician's chair it might be more legible. A speaker who bellows might be more audible: 'But a good speaking voice is one which is inaudible as a voice. I need not warn you that if you begin listening to the inflections and speaking rhythms of a voice from a platform, you are falling asleep.'

Likewise with printing. 'The most important thing,' Warde said, 'is that it conveys thought, ideas, images, from one mind to other minds. This statement is what you might call the front door of the science of typography.'

She explained that the book typographer's job was building a window between the reader inside a room and 'that landscape which is the author's words. He may put up a stained-glass window of marvelous beauty, but a failure as a window; that is, he may use some rich superb type like text gothic that is something to be looked at, not through. Or he may work in what I call transparent or invisible typography. I have a book at home, of which I have no visual recollection whatever as far as its typography goes; when I think of it, all

I see is the Three Musketeers and their comrades swaggering up and down the streets of Paris.'

It is easy to agree with Warde as she sits down to big applause. No one wants a book that's hard to read or offends the eye. But her eighty-year-old viewpoint now seems restrictive, and while her theories chide the flashy they do not reward the curious or the experimental. Warde may have been fearful of the effects of new artistic movements on traditional typographic values; if so, this was a form of xenophobia. To deny the idea that type can itself be the message (to deny that it is enough for it to be exciting and arresting) is to deaden excitement and progress. Warde's severe view has long been abandoned, and now the most important questions when selecting or appreciating type have become: Does it fit the role it was intended for? Does it get its message across? And does it add something of beauty to the world?

Albertus

One of the glorious developments since Beatrice Warde's time is how easy it is to change fonts on a screen. See something you've written that isn't reading well? Try it in a new face and it will read differently; it may seem more fluent, more emphatic, less equivocal. No better? Try the one in this paragraph. Albertus. The most expressive font in town.

To view Albertus on a grander, public scale, take a look at the City of London. Wander around the financial districts and you'll see it everywhere: a sharply cut face combining Roman values with individual flair, its subtle serifs (little inky swellings rather than staunch cast legs) ensuring great legibility. Albertus looks slightly theatrical, and at larger sizes its capital B (with its central bar tapering to a fine point), its upper-case O (thin sides with a hugely gawping lopsided central bowl), and its lower-case a (both geometric and childlike in its stencil-style carving) are particularly striking. The large rounded letters are complemented by the narrow horizontal E, F, L and T, which are even more effective when doubled. The S has a smaller counter at the bottom than at the top, which can make it appear upside-down.

The City can be a windswept unwelcoming place, not least in the evenings and at weekends when the security barriers and all that concrete deadens the soul. Signage becomes particularly important at these times, and Albertus is as welcoming as street furniture can be. It may even help you find the Barbican arts centre, the precise location of which has foxed visitors for decades.

Albertus was created by Berthold Wolpe, the bohemian and reassuringly chaotic designer best remembered for his book jacket designs at Faber & Faber, where his often purely typographic work became as treasured as Faber jackets featuring Edward Bawden, Rex Whistler and Paul Nash. Wolpe learned his craft in Germany, but he fled the Nazis in the mid-1930s and arrived in England to find his services much in demand. In 1980, at the age of seventy-five, he was honoured with a retrospective at the Victoria and Albert Museum, and the display cases within held his dazzling jackets for TS Eliot, Thom Gunn and Robert Lowell (it was estimated he designed at least 1,500).

Wolpe began working on Albertus in 1932 and it swiftly appeared on book jackets, announcing the young Seamus Heaney and William Golding as writers too good to ignore. Before Wolpe, literary novelists and poets had seldom been such visual sensations, their names taking up half the jacket; no wonder they loved him so much.

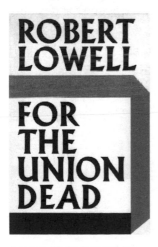

A classic Wolpe Faber jacket

Like Gill Sans, Albertus had its roots not on the drawing board but in the real world – in this case, bronze memorial tablets. Wolpe had enjoyed his formal training in a

Albertus on CD and live in the City of London

bronze foundry, where he learned to compose raised inscriptions, cutting away metal surrounding the letters with a chisel to form a necessary, simple and bold alphabet, something he called 'sharpness without spikiness'.

If the V&A show passed you by, perhaps you noticed Albertus on the CD cover of Coldplay's **PARACHUTES**, or on a DVD re-run of cult TV show *The Prisoner*, the battle between mind-control and individualism. Why Albertus for the show's signs? Because it looked visually stunning, was perfectly suited to the unnerving psychological landscape (the old Roman world on its side), and because – even on small screens in 1960s living rooms – it was brilliantly and crucially legible.

Can a font make me popular?

4

When Matthew Carter arrived for drinks at a private club in Leicester Square in May 2009, he was accompanied by his girlfriend Arlene Chung, and they started talking about films they might see together on their brief visit to London. Carter, a Brit long based in the US, had travelled from his home in Boston to see his children, and to give a lecture about revivals – the process of updating typefaces from the previous five hundred years to suit today's needs. He was such a popular draw that his talk had to be switched to a larger venue.

The lecture was not difficult for Carter. Now in his early seventies, the subject had occupied all his working life. But the choice of movie was more of an issue. It wasn't the subject matter as much as the accuracy – so often when Carter sees films he notices niggly things wrong with type. How could a story set in Peru in the nineteenth century possibly have a sign on a restaurant door that had been composed in Univers from 1957? How could the film *Ed Wood*, set in the 1950s, use Chicago, a font from the 1980s, as the sign at the entrance of a studio? And how did the props team of a movie set at the start of the Second World War get the idea that it would be okay to print a document in Snell Roundhand Bold, when Carter, watching in the multiplex, would recognize the face as something he himself created in 1972?

Carter finds this sort of anomaly more amusing than annoying, but others take it more seriously, and bad type in film upsets them as much as bad continuity. On a section of his website called Typecasting, the designer Mark Simonson has set up a scoring system to denote just how badly filmmakers have got it wrong. He begins with *Chocolat*, the movie in which Juliette Binoche opens up a *chocolaterie* to bring joy to a sleepy 1950s French village. But the local mayor is no fan of type: pinning up a notice preventing the consumption of all but bread and tea during Lent, he has jumped forward a couple of decades to select a typeface (ITC Benguiat) not made until the late 1970s.

Inevitably, this sort of thing happens all the time. The Steve Martin film *Dead Men Don't Wear Plaid*, set in the 1940s, gets three out of five stars for historical accuracy – shame about the use of Blippo from the 1970s for the cruise brochure. *The Hudsucker Proxy*, directed by the Coen Brothers, also gets three stars, despite its studied period feel (beatniks, hula hoops), being marred for type

Fine film, nice brochure, shame about the anachronistic font

fans by a corporate logo set in Bodega Sans from 1991. *LA Confidential* (two stars) fares worse, not least because the nameplate of Danny DeVito's gossip rag *Hush Hush* looks suspiciously like Helvetica Compressed from 1974.

These are modern films, appearing at the cinema at about the same time as graphic design was becoming all the rage at art school. You could sit in the stalls and not only know that something was wrong with a magazine nameplate, but also say why – too ornate, too recent, overly wrought. And we have recently begun to say not only what works, but what we like. 'In the past,' Matthew Carter observes, 'people who had a very well-defined sense of taste in what they wore or what they drove, didn't really have any way of expressing their taste in type. But now you can say, "I prefer Bookman to Palatino" and people do have feelings about it.'

Carter's own taste is for suitability, and for meeting the expectations of his employers. He is not only one of the most highly respected type designers, but one of the few able to make a decent living from the trade. He is proud of a description in a *New Yorker* profile that tagged him as the most widely read man in the world. 'A bit of an exaggeration,' he reasoned, 'but it got people interested.' Carter is also one of the most eloquent exponents of his craft. He looks a bit like his type, a classicist with a ponytail.

He is the creator, notably, of Verdana, whose adoption by Microsoft and Google has given it huge reach; of Georgia, the most legible and adaptable screen font; *Snell Roundhand*, based on an eighteenth-century calligraphic style, very festive, good for ironic party invitations; Bell Centennial, designed for the 100th Bell (now AT&T) phonebook; ITC Galliard, a revival from the sixteenth century, tall and airy; and Tahoma, which, in its Arabic and Thai versions, is used by IKEA in place of its regular font – Verdana. The calligrapher Gunnlaugur SE Briem has described Bell Centennial as 'a bulletproof rhinoceros that could dance *Swan Lake*', and the same could be said for almost all of Carter's work.

There are at least twenty other Carter fonts, and his clients have included the *New York Times* and the *International Herald Tribune*, *Time* and *Newsweek*, the *Washington Post* and the *Guardian*. Beyond this, his work is on almost every computer in the world, and on perhaps half the western world's advertising.

'At one time I dreaded that moment at dinner parties when people asked me what I did,' Carter says. 'Or when I sit next to a stranger on a plane. I was always tempted to pretend that I was a brain surgeon just to avoid the whole topic. Twenty years ago, no one had the slightest idea what a type designer was. If they had miraculously heard of it, they would say things like, "Oh, I thought they were all dead."'

Nowadays, Carter believes, it would be very hard to find anybody over the age of six who didn't know what a font was. 'However, they don't realize any human agency is involved, because fonts for them are part of the software ether that appears mysteriously on their computer, manifestations of some ghostly form. So they're very astonished when they hear that people do this.

'I've had some very funny encounters with people since I've done a number of faces for Microsoft. Microsoft gave them away, which means they are everywhere on the planet. So now people say things like, "Do you know this thing called Verdana? We've just had a memo come around the office saying we've all got to start using it ..." In some companies it's dragooned that they all have to use it so no one thinks

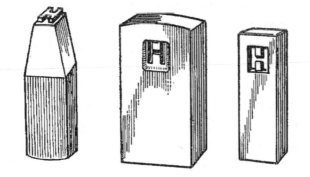

The old tools of the trade: a punch, strike and matrix

they're getting any advantage by sucking up to the boss by using his favourite typeface.'

Occasionally people will ask Carter, 'What typeface should I choose if I want to be really friendly? Can a font make me popular?' He tells them he doesn't know, that he's at the raw material end of this, and that it's all subjective anyhow. And it's too easy to say heavy bold gothic types are serious, gloomy and sad, while light, flouncy, ornate ones resembling human script are optimistic and joyous. He has learned over the years that there is truth in all of this, but he has also learned that it is easier to say what works than why. Good type is instinct born of experience.

Carter's life in type is unusual and instructive. He has worked in three key areas of the craft. His father, Harry, was a typographer and historian, and he helped find his son an unpaid traineeship at Enschedé, since the beginning of the eighteenth century a leading banknote printer and type foundry in the Netherlands. Here he learned to become a punchcutter, and the process of cutting letters in steel taught him about the beauty of the alphabet.

Carter then returned to London, and found there wasn't much demand for skills rooted in the 1450s. So he began to paint signs, another archaic art. At the beginning of the 1960s he went to New York, and his journey into modern typography began. (Technically speaking, typography is concerned with the appearance of type on a page or screen, while type design is concerned principally with the form of the letters.) After a while he was offered a job at the Mergenthaler Linotype Company in Brooklyn, the leading supplier of typesetting machines, and he set about improving their type library.

His subsequent career took him naturally into the new processes of phototypesetting and designing for the computer. In 1981 he co-founded Bitstream Inc, the first significant digital type foundry, and a decade later he left to form Carter & Cone with his business partner Cherie Cone. It was here that he was commissioned – newspaper by newspaper, typeface by typeface – to establish the new look of much of what we currently read in print and online.

Businesses and institutions employ Carter because there aren't many font designers who have such an intricate knowledge of type history. For a man specializing in revivals this is obviously a prerequisite – and it is an attribute often lacking in the generation that followed him. Computers have obliterated the manual labour of casting letters by hand, but

Harry Carter (left) and a young Matthew Carter punchcutting

it is not just the craft that has disappeared; it may be the rounded worldview that such craft brings. Carter says he once went to a fair where someone was offering a poster from the 1840s advertising a forthcoming sale of slaves. He knew immediately it was a fake – its typeface originated from the 1960s. Once again, type can tell you much more than words on a page.

Where did Matthew Carter's knowledge begin? With his mother, who just loved the shape of letters. Before he went to school and learned to read or write, his mother had cut out the alphabet from linoleum. She had trained as an architect, and drew beautifully. Many years later, he found the remains of these letters in a box. 'They were Gill Sans,' Carter says, 'and they had tooth marks on them.'

Futura v Verdana

At the end of August 2009, an unusual thing happened in the world: IKEA changed its typeface. This wasn't so strange in itself – big companies like to stay looking fresh, and this is often the easiest way to do it – but the odd thing was that people noticed.

Most customers didn't like the switch. There was rudeness on websites. Newspapers wrote about it in cutting ways, and there were frank exchanges on BBC radio. It wasn't a revolution on the scale of Gutenberg's printing press, but it did mark a turning point, one of those moments when a lot of people found they cared about something they had never cared about before.

One walked around IKEA and felt a little queasy – or rather, queasier than normal. The place still sold cheapish stuff with Swedish names, the restaurant still offered meatballs, and the IKEA sign was still up there on the side of the building in its yellow and blue proprietary IKEA logo. But there was something unfamiliar about the signage and catalogue. IKEA had abandoned its elegant typeface **Futura** in favour of the modern **Verdana**, and the switch had caused consternation not only among type geeks, but real people. Suddenly there was a font war.

Font wars are usually little spats among the *cognoscenti* and very welcome, too; they generate publicity and informed debate. But this war had spilled out beyond its normal narrow confines. Not so long ago, the talk in the IKEA queue was predominantly about scented tea-lights: they seem great value at first, but they tend not to burn for very long. But in August 2009, people began talking about their love of one typeface and distrust of another.

A few months before, at a corporate meeting in IKEA headquarters in Älmhult, the Swedish furniture company had decided that a move to Verdana would be advantageous. IKEA's decision was chiefly about using the same typeface in print that they used on their website: at the time, Verdana was one of very few 'web-safe fonts' (though, ironically, less than a year later, Futura too was available as a webfont), and it had been designed specifically for use in small sizes on the web (one reason why it draws so much ire in IKEA's usage is that it looks ungainly at large sizes – it wasn't meant to be used large and hi-res).

For many months this decision didn't raise an eyebrow, but then the new catalogues started arriving on type designers' doormats (Thud! The new Ektorp Tullsta armchair cover only £49!!), and instead of looking industrial and tough, the catalogue looked a little more crafted and generously rounded. It also looked a little less like a Scandinavian enterprise founded on the promise of original design, and a bit more like a sales brochure from a company you wouldn't think twice about (a company that has become part of the furniture).

As a result, the members of online discussion groups found they had a new hot topic in their forums. Some were just plaintive: 'So predictable, so dull, so corporate, so please bring back Futura!' And some were clever and funny: 'The round forms in Futura's O really mimicked the Swedish meatballs before. Now we're left ... yearning for the glory days when IKEA embraced continuity between their typography and meat products.'

The arguments showcased the classic battleground of font warfare: new type, old type; a pure intention versus an Evil Empire; an old company seen to be deserting its roots for financial gain; a supremely beautiful typeface battling against a supremely functional one. But this time, they had the ear of the media. The *New York Times* joked that it was 'perhaps the

Futura (top) gives way to Verdana

biggest controversy to ever come out of Sweden'. Wikipedia wasted no time in accepting a new page called Verdanagate. It became the hot topic – a fontroversy – in Graphic Tweets. The passion some people displayed when it came to type seemed tribal, like the passion of sports fans.

The two fonts in question had much to do with this. Futura (of which more later) has a quirkiness to it that Verdana does not, with a pedigree linked to political art movements of the 1920s. Verdana, on the other hand, despite being a superb font, designed by Matthew Carter, is linked to something modern and commonly reviled: Microsoft. Verdana is thus available on almost every PC and Mac, and is one of the most widely used fonts in the world. Along with a handful of other prominent typefaces, it has been directly responsible for a homogenization of the public word: a sign over a cinema looks increasingly like one over a bank or hospital, and magazines that once looked original now frequently resemble something designed for reading online. This is what had happened at IKEA: the new look had been defined not by a company proudly parading its sixty-six year heritage, but by economies of scale and the demands of the digital age.

Nothing wrong with that; it's a business. A new font is unlikely to have a detrimental effect on sales; what should we care if the label describing the Billy Bookcase is Futura, Verdana or Banana so long as the price is right? Like the bookcase, Verdana was also in almost every home, and becoming something you barely noticed. But that, for dissenters, was the point: Verdana was everywhere, and now it was in one more place. It was becoming a non-font that we don't even register. Which is precisely why it was so effective, and exactly why it was chosen.

The HANDS of UNLETTERED MEN

In 1969 Matthew Carter's father Harry published a book called *A View of Early Typography Up to About 1600*. It is not exactly a page-turner, but it was well crafted in Monotype Bembo and it explored a crucial element of our literary past. And Harry Carter was a man who knew his type. Initially a barrister, he turned to design and learned to print, engrave, to cut punches (he made a Hebrew text while on military service in Palestine), and after the war became chief designer at His Majesty's Stationery Office.

As a historian, Carter was particularly interested in the bountiful fifteenth-century collision between, on the one hand, the burgeoning technological knowledge and abilities of typefounders and printers, and on the other, the clamouring demands from publishers and the reading public. A map of Europe at the end of the book shows the sites of printing in Europe in 1476, and the map is busy: just twenty years since Gutenberg, there are books and pamphlets running off presses in Oxford, Antwerp, Strasbourg, Lubeck, Rostock, Nuremberg, Geneva, Lyons, Toulouse, Milan, Rome, Naples and about forty other towns and cities. Even secret knowledge travelled fast: every court and university demanded not just the latest publications but also the means of producing them. With matrices, moulds and type, there was suddenly a new commodity on the market, and the centre of trade and the heart of printing was Venice.

In Venice, more than fifty printers competed for the passing merchant's attention, and clarity was a strong selling point. The da Spira brothers from Germany established their Venetian type in the city in the 1460s, a flowing and orderly face that broke away entirely from the gothic weights of Gutenberg, Schoeffer and Fust: it is easily readable to us

Easy reading: Venetian typesetting from the da Spira brothers (left) and Nicholas Jenson

today, the eye gliding rather than snagging along it, the first truly modern printed font. In the 1470s a Venetian scribe feared that he would soon be out of business, complaining that his city was 'stuffed with books'. And things would get worse: by the end of the century about 150 presses had produced more than 4,000 different editions – about twice as many as Venice's most proficient rival, Paris.

Not all of the new printers made money, and the quality of their product varied greatly. But it was the fifteenth-century equivalent of the goldrush, and with no restrictions on joining the fray. Erasmus observed that for a while it was easier to become a printer than a baker.

The greatest single expense was production of the metal type, which was already a truly international commodity. Styles were refined in Venice by Nicolas Jenson, a Frenchman who had travelled to Mainz in 1458, where he had probably picked up Gutenberg's techniques but rejected the more impenetrable elements of his Gothic output. But Jenson's classical Venetian – strong and stately with thick slab serifs – was only a stepping stone for the great modern breakthrough to come.

Fifteen years after Jenson's death, his work was lightened and rounded by the Italian 'old face' of Aldus Manutius, the humanist publisher credited with inventing the semi-colon, and establishing the modern book trade with his easily transportable pocket-sized versions of Greek philosophy and literary Latin – the ancient texts that illuminated the Italian High Renaissance.

Many of the types for these books were in fact cut by the goldsmith Francesco Griffo. It was Griffo who created the ancestor of the classic Bembo font – which he devised to set a brief account of a trip to Mount Etna by a Venetian cardinal of the name – and, around 1500, introduced italic type – not as a method of highlighting text but of setting entire books in a more condensed form.*

Not everyone approved of these new types, nor the use to which they were put. A stroll from the Rialto to San Marco now offered a world of knowledge previously unavailable, and affordable books in Greek and Latin were joined by vernacular and Roman texts that told of concepts both intellectual and erotic. The bestsellers were no longer just religious, they were the opposite – lustful texts by Virgil and Ovid. Even those who had previously advocated the printed dissemination of wisdom complained of dumbing down: Hieronimo Squarciafico, who worked with Manutius, feared that the 'abundance of books makes men less studious', and he dreamed of a scenario in Elysian Fields in which great authors bemoaned that 'printing had fallen into the hands of unlettered men, who corrupted almost everything'. Of particular concern was the digested read and the accessible history – knowledge falling within the hands of those who had previously regarded it as being beyond their reach.

The phrase 'the fount of all knowledge' originated around this time, and there are two possible derivations. It was thought that a single fount or font could now reveal everything that was known. Or a fount could have been

* Manutius and Griffo later fell out, and there were squabbles over who was responsible for the first italic types. It is widely believed that the inspiration stemmed from the hand of Niccolo Niccoli, a contemporary Venetian who used a slanted style when he wished to write faster or express dynamism. However, punchcutters in Florence also subsequently placed a claim.

short for fountain, as used in a lecture in Venice in 1508 by the mathematician Luca Pacioli. Referring to the fifth book of Euclid's *Elements*, he suggested that readers would surely prosper in the world of arts and sciences if only they heed 'this ever flowing fountain, the knowledge of proportion'.

In London, the merchant William Caxton set up a printing press in Westminster in 1476, after returning from a long stint in Bruges (the first book printed in English is believed to be his publication there of Lefèvre's *Recuyell of the Historyes of Troye* around 1473). Caxton was a practical man, as keen to exploit new developments in communication and commerce as the pioneers of the Internet. He was a proficient translator (the Troy histories was his own work), albeit one aware of his linguistic and typographic shortcomings; he frequently, if perhaps rhetorically, asked his readers 'to correcte and amende where they shal fynde faulte'.

In his *Vocabulary in French and English* (*c.* 1480), Caxton or his compositor not only confused his 'p's and 'q's, but even more frequently muddled his 'b's and 'd's and his 'u's and 'n's, so similar did they appear in his small typefaces. The *Vocabulary* has so many misprints that you feel like writing in disgust to the publisher. In an introduction to the facsimile edition of 1964, the Cambridge under-librarian JCT Oates found 177 errors in French, of which 102 are confusions between u and n, and 38 misprints in English, including 17 mix-ups between u and n in such words as aud, dnchesse and bnt. But Caxton's influence on the standardization of English was considerable, as was his introduction to the language of silent letters (as in Ghent and nought), betraying the Flemish training of some of his letter carvers.

Caxton's type was initially imported from Flanders, though around 1490 he seems to have switched to new fonts cut in Rouen and Paris. We know this from the appearance of a ragged r in place of the old blackletter form – a certain link to French foundries. It was a clear sign too that a popular type matrix was now a regular commodity of trade, boxed in the cargo hold alongside spice, lace, wine and paper.

Caxton's eye for business remained strong. He set up a temporary shop in Westminster to catch the passing trade of members of the House of Lords, selling imported books and manuscripts as well as his own publications. He printed about a hundred works, achieving his greatest success with the *Canterbury Tales*. The many versions of Chaucer's manuscript were so popular among merchants and noble-

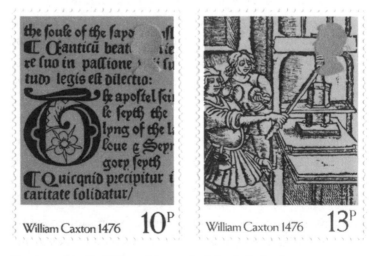

Stamps marking the 500th anniversary of printing in England

men that when Caxton came to set it in type he found that, entirely befitting of a compendium of tall tales, it was hard to locate Chaucer's original. He printed two folios, in 1478 and 1483, each in a typeface that we could mistake for slightly rushed handwriting. They were, however, fonts that showed a burgeoning public taste for a style as far removed from gothic formality as possible.

Caxton was not a great typographer, which was one of the principal reasons he valued Wynkyn de Worde, his young successor at his London press. De Worde was the first known printer on Fleet Street, setting up there around 1500 and employing an expanding range of European typefaces for his increasingly popular output. He exploited the growing demand for cheaper publications, selling Latin grammar texts to schools while also printing novels, poetry, music and illustrated children's books for his bookstand at St Paul's. At the onset of the sixteenth century, his innovations were being imitated throughout Europe, the revolution in movable type delighting the common reader and disgusting the church just fifty years after Gutenberg.

Doves

Good type never dies, but there is one notable exception – Doves, the type that drowned.

Nicholas Jenson's Venetian font has inspired many dignified revivals, but the finest and most elusive was created for the Doves Press in about 1900. Doves Press was established in Hammersmith, west London, by the bookbinder Thomas Cobden-Sanderson. It was named after a nearby pub, but its ambitions were loftier. Cobden-Sanderson said he would not cease until he had designed 'The Book Beautiful'.

William Morris's famous edict to 'have nothing in your home that you do not know to be useful or believe to be beautiful' certainly applied to Doves, although there are few printed art-efacts upon which we may view it. Its most famous application was in the Doves Bible of 1902, set in the traditional typographer's style of black with red trimmings, and possessed of a slightly rickety serif form, as if someone had broken into the press after hours and banged into the compositor's plates.

The type was cut in London by Edward Prince, who had earlier made typefaces for William Morris at the Kelmscott Press (notably his Golden Type of 1891, a lavish, weighty and flowery reaction to the cleaner, modern lines of the day). The hand-drawn

IN THE BEGINNING

GOD CREATED THE HEAVEN AND THE EARTH. ⁋AND THE EARTH WAS WITHOUT FORM, AND VOID; AND DARKNESS WAS UPON THE FACE OF THE DEEP, & THE SPIRIT OF GOD MOVED UPON THE FACE OF THE WATERS. ⁋And God said, Let there be light: & there was light. And God saw the light, that it was good: & God divided the light from the darkness. And God called the light Day, and the darkness he called Night. And the evening and the morning were the first day. ⁋And God said, Let there be a firmament in the midst of the waters, & let it divide the waters from the waters. And God made the firmament, and divided the waters which were under the firmament from the waters which were above the firmament: & it was so. And God called the firmament Heaven. And the evening & the morning were the second day. ⁋And God said, Let the waters under the heaven be gathered together unto one place, and let the dry land appear: and it was so. And God called the dry land Earth; and the gathering together of the waters called he Seas: and God saw that it was good. And God said, Let the earth bring forth grass, the herb yielding seed, and the fruit tree yielding fruit after his kind, whose seed is in itself, upon the earth: & it was so. And the earth brought forth grass, & herb yielding seed after his kind, & the tree yielding fruit, whose seed was in itself, after his kind: and God saw that it was good. And the evening & the morning were the third day. ⁋And God said, Let there be lights in the firmament of the heaven to divide the day from the night; and let them be for signs, and for seasons, and for days, & years: and let them be for lights in the firmament of the heaven to give light upon the earth: & it was so. And God made two great lights; the greater light to rule the day, and the lesser light to rule the night: he made the stars also. And God set them in the firmament of the heaven to give light upon the earth, and to rule over the day and over the night, & to divide the light from the darkness: and God saw that it was good. And the evening and the morning were the fourth day. ⁋And God said, Let the waters bring forth abundantly the moving creature that hath life, and fowl that may fly above the earth in the open firmament of heaven. And God created great whales, & every living creature that moveth, which the waters brought forth abundantly, after their kind, & every winged fowl after his kind: & God saw that it was good. And God blessed them, saying, Be fruitful, & multiply, and fill the waters in the seas, and let fowl multiply in the earth. And the evening & the morning were the fifth day. ⁋And God said, Let the earth bring forth the living creature after his kind, cattle, and creeping thing, and beast of the earth after his kind: and it was so. And God made the beast of the earth after his kind, and cattle after their kind, and every thing that creepeth upon the

27

Doves Bible – Cobden-Sanderson's masterpiece

text on the first page of the Bible ('IN THE BEGINNING') was drawn by Edward Johnston, the calligrapher who would go on to design the type for the London Underground.

Doves type is most easily recognized by its ample space between letters, a y that descends without a curl, a ligature connecting c and t, and the bottom bowl of its g set at an angle, giving it a sense of motion, like a helicopter tilting at take-off. Edward Gorey and Tim Burton appeared to lean on it gratefully for their hand-drawn text.

Doves has another reason for notoriety besides its beauty. When Cobden-Sanderson split from his partner Emery Walker

Cobden-Sanderson photographed with his future wife Annie and her sister Jane, with Jane Morris (wife of William Morris), on a visit to Sienna in 1881.

and the Doves Press dissolved in 1908, the pair drew up a legal agreement that Cobden-Sanderson would own the type (which meant all the punches and matrices) until his death, after which it would pass to Walker. But then Cobden-Sanderson changed his mind Fearing its use both in shoddy printing and undesirable subject matter, he took the entire letter fund to Hammersmith Bridge and threw it in the Thames.

Was this an impetuous act? Rather the opposite. Cobden-Sanderson thought about it for weeks, planning both its execution and purpose. His Last Will and Testament contained details of how he would 'bequeath' Doves type to the river, so it may be washed 'to and from the great sea for ever and for ever'. His motive was not entirely aesthetic – it was also bloody-minded. Doves was his creation and he resented his partner.

Cobden-Sanderson first dispatched the matrices – the casts for the type. But that was the easy part: disposing of the metal letters themselves would take him three more years. The war had made him despondent and unwell, but his own destructive force seldom receded. 'I had gone for a stroll on the Mall,' he wrote in his diary at the end of August 1916, 'when it occurred to me that it was a suitable night and time; so I went indoors, and taking first one page and then two, succeeded in destroying three. I will now go on until I have destroyed the whole of it.'

These pages were solid blocks of type, just as they had been used to print the last Doves book. As the weeks went on, he would take as many blocks as he could manage, wrap them in paper tied with string, walk about half a mile from his press to the best spot, and drop them into the water after nightfall, often waiting for heavy traffic to obscure the sound of the splash.

Over the next five months, he made more than a hundred separate trips to the bridge with his type, a large undertaking for a frail man of seventy-six. And it was not without hitches. 'On Friday night I threw two packets of type from the bridge,' he noted in November 1916, 'but they alighted one after the other on a projecting level ledge of the southernmost pier, and there remain, visible, inaccessible, irremovable by me.'

Cobden-Sanderson feared discovery – 'by the police, the public, the newspapers!' – but escaped detection to the very end, until, after his death, his will and diary were discovered. Emery Walker, for one, was not amused and started legal proceedings against Cobden-Sanderson's wife, Annie, a militant Suffragette (and daughter of the radical Liberal reformer, Richard Cobden). He said he had made some attempt to have the whole font re-cut, but Edward Prince had lost his touch and Walker could find no one else who could do it justice. The case was settled out of court, Annie Cobden-Sanderson agreeing to pay £700. Doves was never recovered, at least not the full alphabet. Even now it seems likely that the disintegrating typeface is stuck firm in the riverbed, resisting both dredging and the digital age, perhaps occasionally breaking free to form its own words and sentences as fortune and the molten tide allows.

The Ampersand's
Final Twist

6

Much of what one needs to know about the history and beauty of a font may be found in its ampersand. Done well, an & is not so much a character as a creature, an animal from the deep. Or it is a character in the other sense of the word, usually a tirelessly entertaining one, perhaps an uncle with too many magic tricks.

Although long treated as a single character or glyph, the ampersand is actually two letters combined – the e and the t of the Latin 'et' (the word ampersand is a conflation of 'et, per se and'). It is the result of scribes working fast: its first use is usually credited to a shorthand writing method proposed by Marcus Tiro in 63 BC.

The finest ampersand, cut by William Caslon, is still alive after almost three hundred years, and it has many impersonators but no equals. It is fiendishly difficult to draw, and when done badly may resemble aimless scribble. But when done well, it can be a work of wild freehand art in a way that few regular characters are allowed to be. It can bestow aristocratic virtue to a font, and it can cause the writer about fonts a considerable struggle to contain the purple prose.

Aldus Manutius was particularly keen on the ampersand and used some twenty-five of them on a single page of his *Hypnerotomachia Poliphili* of 1499. They don't have the beauty of Caslon's symbol, but Manutius's font-cutter, Griffo, came up with a character remarkably similar to the ones that gained favour in the last century and are in common use today.

For the first real flight of fancy, we need to look to that revolutionary Frenchman, Claude Garamond, the man who instilled the virtues of clear roman type on sixteenth-century Paris. With the ampersand, however, he allowed himself

to head off from type to art. His character provides a clear indication of the form's origin: on the left side the e, on the right the t. But they are linked by a cradle that begins weightily then thins out, and there are inky globular endings to each end of the crossbar on the t.

Claude Garamond ...

This & That

... and his italicized ampersand

It betrays strong calligraphic roots, but what distinguishes it is the ascending stroke on the e portion, something that begins in the regular way as a belt across the letter, before ascending freely skywards, resembling the darting tongue of a lizard catching flies. It must have been great fun to sketch; painfully difficult to cut in metal.

Garamond's types became the most popular in Europe for the best part of two hundred years. The ampersand, the Q and the 'double V' setting of the W are the only characters that we would regard as fancy today, while the rest of it just looks clean, and sparklingly personable. There are a great many re-cut foundry variations, but in almost all of them the alphabet has a fine and open appeal, with a confident serif and stroke variation, particularly noticeable on the middle bars of E and F. It is most easily identifiable by the very small bowl of the lower-case e. It does have a plain, primitive and unsophisticated aspect but Garamond's conscious mastery of technique ensures it remains the most popular early font in the pull-down computer menu.

We classify Garamond's fonts as 'old-face', but when they emerged at the behest of François I in the 1540s, they marked a final transition from gothic letters to the roman alphabet we recognize today, refining the work a century earlier of Manutius and the Venetians. Like the work of his fellow

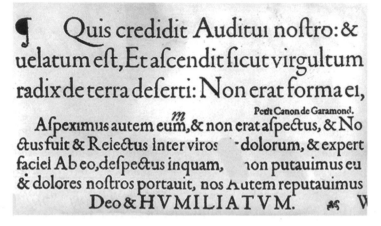

A specimen page of Garamond's original font

Frenchman Jenson, these were not types masquerading as manuscript but type on its own terms. The alphabet is full of contrast and movement but with a precision of line and elegant serifs, so even today, if you want something respectable yet warm, a Garamond is a fine choice. In fact, Garamond may be the first typeface many of us encounter, being used for the Dr Seuss books and the US editions of *Harry Potter*.

England had to wait almost two hundred years for a type designer to rival Garamond. William Caslon's fonts from the 1720s may have had less of a lasting impact, in that they are less visible in current usage, but they were no less significant in their establishment of a strong English style: confident serifs, heavy capitals in comparison to the lower case, an important wide M grounding the alphabet from the centre.

Caslon may have modelled his types on those of the Antwerp printer Plantin, and his French typefounder Robert Granjon, and a part of their appeal was that they were specifically not German. Depending on the quality of printing and bleed of the ink, the whole alphabet could also display a vaguely piratical cragginess.

It's no surprise to find that Caslon himself began as a gunsmith, engraving rifles with fancy swirls and initials, and he maintained these flourishes on his 'swash' capitals (capitals with elaborate loops and tails, usually for the first and last letter of a word). But his ampersand seemed to come from an altogether more hallucinogenic place, from the playground perhaps, or from the alehouse.

The finest example available today is the version supplied by the International Typeface Corporation – the ITC 540 Caslon Italic. This is practically a meal in itself, with a matronly e threatening to engulf the t, the two in perennial conflict over which has the dandiest loops. It suggests a creator delighting in new freedoms after the repressions of strict Ts and Vs. Caslon's ampersand makes an impressive T-shirt, intriguingly handsome to passers-by, occasionally eliciting a nod from another aficionado, like smug fans of a cool pop band before it becomes famous. (Hearteningly, the Caslon business is still going strong, and still family run. It now offers such things as digital press feeders and FoilTech supplies.)

Caslon's ampersand, looking
good on a MyFonts T-shirt

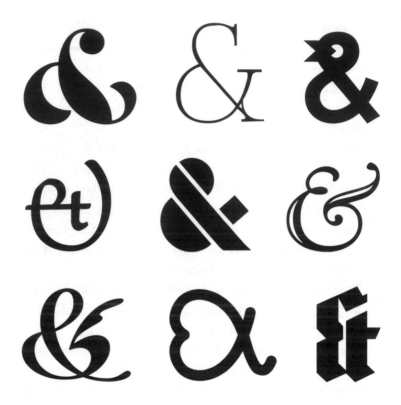

Ampersand madness – the Coming Together charity project

The ampersand travels well abroad, carrying the same meaning without need for 'und' in German, 'e' in Italian and Portuguese and 'og' in Danish and Norwegian. Occasionally it can go astray: it is the one element of Albertus that looks odd and too roughly hewn, and the ugly Univers version looks as if it was drawn by committee. Eric Gill argued that the ampersand was far too handy to be employed merely in business literature (as was usual), although he then tended to overuse it in his essays where just a plain 'and' would suffice (it doesn't always look great in 12pt text).

Even in its more basic modern form, the ampersand is far more than abbreviation; its creativity provides a heartening reminder of the continuing impact of the quill in type design, and it signifies more than just a link. It also signifies permanence, not least to a professional partnership; Dean & Deluca are clearly in it for the long haul, as are Ben & Jerry's, Marks & Spencer and the magazines *House & Garden* and *Town & Country*. But Simon and Garfunkel? No wonder they kept splitting up. Tom and Jerry? Of course they hate each other.

The biggest and most noble demonstration of its unifying potential came in early 2010, when the Society of Typographic Aficionados (SOTA) released 'Coming Together', a font consisting of 483 different ampersands. This cost $20, with all proceeds going to Doctors Without Borders to assist with the Haiti Earthquake appeal. Almost four hundred designers from thirty-seven countries contributed one or more glyphs, ranging from the Caslon-esque to the almost unrecognizable. It was the fourth FontAid event, the first three benefiting Unicef (26 letter pairs), the families of victims of September 11 (a collection of question marks) and those affected by the Indian Ocean earthquake and tsunami (400 floral ornaments known as fleurons).

Coming Together swiftly became a bestseller at the digital font agencies that offered it. This is the best thing about the ampersand – its energy, its refusal to sit still. It is almost impossible to look at one and not think about its shape, or to draw one and not think about liberation.

7
Baskerville is Dead
(Long Live Baskerville)

In October 1775, a German physicist and hunchback named Georg Christoph Lichtenberg travelled across Europe to visit one John Baskerville of Birmingham, only to find that he had died the previous January. It was a cruel disappointment: Lichtenberg had hoped to meet the man he considered the pre-eminent type designer of his age.

Baskerville worked chiefly as a japanner – someone who made objects with decorative lacquer – and as an engraver of headstones. But his passion was for printing and letter making. Oddly, considering Baskerville is one of the great names of type history, he met with little success in his lifetime. His books – notably his editions of Virgil and *Paradise Lost* – were works of art with huge flaws. His paper was too shiny and the texts were peppered with corrections ('like the crossings of a schoolboy,' one critic observed).

But Baskerville's fonts were, for their time, unusually slender, delicate, well balanced and tasteful. They appeared modern, though type historians would now classify them as 'Transitional', an eighteenth-century bridge between Caslon's slightly heavier 'English Old' face and the 'Modern' hairline artistry of French typefounders Didot.

Baskerville and his punchcutter John Handy produced a single basic font in several sizes and forms, and it has one attribute that makes it infallibly recognizable and timelessly stunning – the upper-case Q. This has a tail extending well beyond its body width, a great flourish seldom seen beyond calligraphy. The lower-case g is also a classic with its curled ear and its lower bowl left unclosed, as if all the ink was being saved for that Q.

Baskerville's M and N have traditional bracketed serifs, the oval O is conventionally thicker at its sides than at its top and bottom. But by the time Baskerville came round to designing the Q he may have been getting restless. So the squirrelish tail flits a little to the left and then much further to the right, varying its thickness as it does so. In words such as Queen and Quest, the tail almost underlines the u, cupping it with tenderness.

Georg Lichtenberg would have used the Baskerville Q in the word Quire, for amongst his many interests (hydrogen ballooning, the patterns of tree branches) was the standardization of European paper sizes. His ill-timed journey from his university in Gottingen to Baskerville's

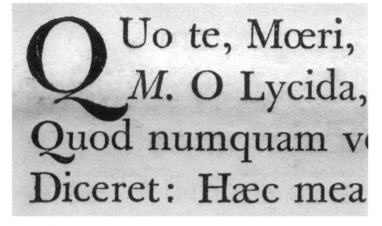

The Baskerville Q in all its glory

house in the English Midlands had been encouraged by King George III. Lichtenberg had taken the King on a tour of the Royal Observatory, and when the two began discussing books, George expressed an interest in Baskerville. Lichtenberg was also encouraged by Johannes Christian Dieterich, a German publisher and bookseller and another fan of Baskerville's work. He wrote to Dieterich from St Paul's Coffee House on his return to London, and conveyed the grim news:

> Only on my arrival did I learn that he was buried more than six months ago. I waited on his widow, an excellent woman, who is continuing the type-foundry, but has almost certainly given up the printing press.

In one sense, Lichtenberg arrived at the perfect moment. Baskerville's wife Sarah was conducting the eighteenth-century equivalent of a car boot sale. He found her to be a grieving woman in fabulous black mourning silks, but not averse to giving the visitor a full tour of the works. 'She accompanied me herself into all the most dirty nooks of the type-foundry,' Lichtenberg wrote to Dieterich. 'I saw the punches and matrices for all the elegant letters which we have so often admired.'

Sarah Baskerville 'took no pleasure in such a life,' he reported, and wanted rid of it. 'She is willing to sell her whole printing equipment, with all punches, matrices, and everything appertaining to the type-foundry ... for £4,000, her husband formerly having been offered £5,000.' Lichtenberg noted that this even included free delivery to London. 'What a chance, if only one had the money: just fancy the type that might be cast from the existing moulds and the moulds that might be struck with the existing punches; it is a transaction which would either make a man's fortune or bankrupt him.'

It was a valid point. Even after it was cut, a metal typeface needed lavish care and expenditure. The metal would wear out and break, a particular problem with the fine vertical lines in Baskerville; this would necessitate a recasting with the original moulds. Then the paper had to be right (Baskerville introduced 'wove' paper with no watermark and a uniform surface), and the ink had to be the correct consistency to ensure adhesion and clarity, and then there was binding and marketing to consider. And Baskerville was an innovator as well: his wooden presses made a shallower impression, and his inks were blacker and dried more quickly. Despite his endeavours, and the finesse of his fonts, Baskerville often complained that they did not pay. He found that users would copy them rather than buy them: 'Had I no other dependence than typefounding and printing,' he observed in 1762, 'I must starve.' Contemporary type designers might complain that not much has changed. Nonetheless, the Baskerville font has been in extensive and more or less continuous use for the past 250 years.

But who was he, this genius of type, whose widow was merrily flogging his great passion? Opinions vary. According to Baskerville's own account of himself, he was a man slightly possessed. 'Among the several mechanic Arts that have engaged my attention,' he wrote in the preface to his edition of *Paradise Lost*, 'there is no one which I have pursued with so much steadiness and pleasure as that of Letter Founding. Having been an early admirer of the beauty of letters, I became insensibly desirous of contributing to the perfection of them.'

Some considered Baskerville's ambitions realized from the outset, with Lord Macaulay noting that his work 'went forth to astonish all the libraries of Europe'. The Parisian typefounder Pierre Simon Fournier, who promoted the idea of the point sizing system for type, noted of Baskerville's faces that 'he has spared neither pains nor expense to bring them to the utmost pitch of perfection. The letters are cut with great daring and the italic is the best to be found in any English foundry, but the roman is a little too wide.'

In 1760 Baskerville's friend Benjamin Franklin wrote to him from London of a 'pleasant instance of the prejudice some have entertained against your work'. Franklin, an industrious printer around Fleet Street who popularized the use of Baskerville fonts in the United States before pursuing his more scientific and constitutional ambitions, had met a man who said, 'You would be a means of blinding all the readers of the nation, for the strokes of your letters being too thin and narrow, hurt the eye, and he could never read a line of them without pain.'

John Baskerville, painted shortly before his death

Franklin tried to support Baskerville against this charge, but in vain. 'You see this gentleman was a connoisseur.' But then Franklin paid a trick on him. He gave him type specimens apparently printed in Baskerville, and the man in question again detected a 'painful disproportion'. In fact, Franklin had given him texts printed only in Caslon. (Despite the emergence of Baskerville, and Franklin's enthusiastic promotion of it when he returned to the United States, the first mass-produced printing of the Declaration of Independence of 1776 was printed in Caslon.)

A history of Birmingham published in 1835 observed that Baskerville 'was a humourist, idle in the extreme. He could well design, but procured others to execute'. One visitor recalled 'a most profane wretch, and ignorant of literature to a wonderful degree. I have seen many of his letters, which like his will, was not written grammatically, nor could he even spell well.'

In the event, Lichtenberg didn't buy Baskerville's punches and matrices. Instead they passed to Pierre de Beaumarchais, the dramatist responsible for *The Marriage of Figaro* and *The Barber of Seville*, who bought them in 1779 for the Literary and Typographical Society. The society intended to use them to print the complete works of Voltaire in 168 volumes. It is likely that they were also used to produce much revolutionary propaganda in Paris. They were sold again to a French foundry before landing at their current resting place at Cambridge University Press. (Ironically, the first full Baskerville biography, published by CUP in 1907, was printed in Caslon.)

A similar restless fate befell the remains of Baskerville

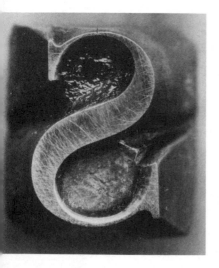

himself. Suspicious of religion, Baskerville had few friends in the church, and had arranged for his own mausoleum to be erected in his grounds. Here he was buried vertically, a further snub to tradition. But he proved a movable type: in 1827, half a century after his death, his body was found by workmen lying horizontally beneath a pile of gravel. He had been shunted

One of Baskerville's punches, cut by John Handy

from his mausoleum by the new owner of the grounds, and apparently just dumped nearby.

When the body was found it was wrapped in a linen shroud covered by sprigs of bay and laurel. His facial skin was described in a local newspaper as 'dry but perfect'. The eyes had gone, but eyebrows, eyelashes, lips and teeth remained. 'An exceedingly offensive and oppressive effluvia strongly resembling decayed cheese arose from the body, and rendered it necessary to close the coffin in a short time.' The newspaper concluded that even in this undignified state he was 'possessed of a natural elegance of taste, which distinguished every thing which came from his hands'.

Following this discovery, he was interred in a catacomb in a Birmingham churchyard, but then moved again when the space made way for shops. He ended up beneath the chapel in Warstone Lane, in a vault that has since been bricked up to deter vandals. This is how we honour our type heroes.

Fortunately, the famous Baskerville typefaces do not rot. They were revived in the 1920s and even before the computer there were a great variety on offer. In the United States in the 1950s Baskerville became a favourite advertising font, not least when a face was required to portray authority and tradition – or something folksy or English.

The names that Baskerville assigned to his types referred to their sizes. They are not in common use today but they would have seemed like family to many generations of compositors and printers: Great Primer, Double Pica Roman Capitals, Brevier Number 1 Roman, Two-Line Double Pica Italic Caps. These days they sound more like complicated orders for coffee, their varieties having been ordered into more familiar mediums and bolds. But every major foundry has long had their own version, tailored specifically for Monotype or Linotype composing machines in the 1920s, and for phototypesetting in the late 1950s. And when the Apple iPad was launched in April 2010, Baskerville was one of the initial five typeface choices available on its iBooks reading device.

Baskerville on the iPad: the other iBook launch fonts were Times New Roman, Palatino, Cochin and Verdana

Mrs Eaves
& Mr Eaves

Mrs Baskerville had been married before, and it was not a happy tale. At the age of sixteen she wed one Richard Eaves, with whom she bore five children, before he deserted her. She was then working as John Baskerville's live-in housekeeper — and later became his lover. But she was unable to marry Baskerville until Eaves's death in 1764 and it may be that some of the society disapproval of Baskerville's work was fired by their unorthodox relationship.

It was a story that intrigued the contemporary type designer Zuzana Licko. 'We were brainstorming for the name of a release,' she recalls, 'and when I mentioned the Mrs Eaves story, the name stuck.' She also remembers reading the criticism Baskerville received from his peers, and 'from experience, I could sympathize.' But when she walks into a bookstore these days and sees how many book covers are designed with Mrs Eaves, she feels pride.

Mrs Eaves, which appeared in 1996, has less variation in its strokes than Baskerville, but maintains its openness and legibility,

Gleeful Romp–Back Alley

THE LOVE LUMP

clasp such cheeky a giggler

Sticky Sweets

in red as beet, *chills to feet*

Chocolate Brown

Aquamarine

LIGHT DELPHINIUM

Reddish Purple

Strawberry

Zuzana Licko's Mrs Eaves (top) and Mr Eaves

as does its more recent sans serif companion, **Mr Eaves**. This is a Baskerville type without the serifs, but still linked to the eighteenth century through its quill-tailed Q, strident R, and the cat-tailed lower bowl of its g, the letters airily spaced and crisp. There is a Mr Eaves Modern version too, which is more geometrical, and might gain approval from John Baskerville for its precision and sophistication, if not its form.

What Baskerville might equally enjoy is a young Australian woman who calls herself Mrs Eaves and likes nothing more than to write all over her body in black marker pen and post the results on YouTube. The most popular video features Mrs Eaves (real name Gemma O'Brien) in gym gear, which leaves a lot of room to inscribe 'Write Here, Right Now' in different letter styles on her flesh, to the accompaniment of the Fatboy Slim song of almost the same name. She sums up her work thus: 'eight hours writing, five marker pens, three baths and two showers'.

Mrs Eaves in action at the Berlin Type Conference

Tunnel Visions

'With care,' the sheet of paper warned at the bottom. 'Ink not waterproof.'

And in this way, in the midst of the First World War, began one of the most iconic, enduring and best-loved fonts in the world, Edward Johnston's type for the London Underground. Within a few years **JOHNSTON SANS** would be visible not only at Elephant & Castle and Golders Green, but at all points where posters were pasted to walls: there was the university boat race at Putney in March, the FA Cup Final at Wembley in May, the fireworks on Hampstead Heath in November; there were the dahlias in St James's Park, the crocuses at Kew, Peter Pan in Kensington Gardens and orators in Hyde Park. Edward Johnston's work adorned every announcement, whether beautiful or grim (THE LAST NORTHBOUND TRAIN HAS GONE).

Johnston was the man who defined London with type, dominating the capital from the far western reaches of the Metropolitan line in Amersham to easterly Upminster on the District line. The blue plaque commemorating his time in Hammersmith remembers him, curiously, as a 'Master calligrapher' rather than the man who signed London, but it is the only plaque to appear in his own type. (Most are in hand-carved antique English fonts with a light serif, akin to what you see on Victorian gravestones.)

Johnston was a gaunt, fine-boned man with a full moustache. To Evelyn Waugh, writing in the *Spectator* in 1959, he was 'a singularly pure and loveable artist' to whom

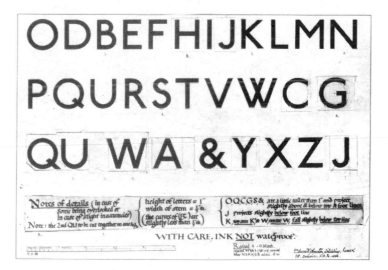

Johnston's original pasted-up designs for the Tube

Edward Johnston at work, complete with high-quality quill and 'tache

we all owe a debt: 'Every schoolboy who learns the italic script, every townsman who reads the announcements of the Underground railway, everyone who studies the maps attached to modern travel books is seeing in the light of Johnston.' Waugh had met Johnston when he was fourteen, the result of winning an art prize. Johnston welcomed him into his workshop in Ditchling in Sussex, and cut a quill from a turkey feather before writing a passage. Waugh recalls a feeling of 'awe and exhilaration'. Eric Gill, one of Johnston's students, was similarly affected.

Johnston himself had studied medicine in Edinburgh, before finding his true calling after examining calligraphy at the British Library. From 1899 he held calligraphy classes at London's Central School of Arts and Crafts, where Gill said he was 'struck as by lightning' by his talents, and remembered the 'thrill and tremble of the heart' as he first experienced Johnston's writing (the two became firm friends, later sharing lodgings). Another admirer, TJ Cobden-Sanderson of Doves Press fame, commissioned Johnston to write out his 'Book Beautiful' manifesto on vellum.

Johnston's **Underground** lettering is often considered the first modern sans, preceding (and possibly inspiring) Jakob Erbar's **Erbar** (1926), Paul Renner's **Futura** (1927) and Rudolf Koch's **Kabel** (1927). **Gill Sans** (1928) certainly owes it an enormous debt, which Eric Gill was happy to acknowledge. It may also be regarded as the first 'people's typeface', the first to be designed for day-to-day use that was not associated with learning, political manifesto or class, but instead with the need to travel. This was type design making a major contribution to society and everyday life. Or as Stanley

Morison – redesigner of *The Times* and a man not given to hyperbole – put it: 'Johnston sans' standardization on the Underground conferred upon it, as lettering, a sanction, civic and commercial, such as had not been accorded to an alphabet since the time of Charlemagne.'

Johnston began working on his underground design in 1915, but the idea had been mooted two years before, when Gerard Meynell, head of the fine-printing house, Westminster Press, which had a contract to produce London Underground posters, introduced Johnston to Frank Pick, the Underground's commercial manager. Pick, an influential figure in British design, had begun to think about a relatively new concept: branding. He had plans not only for the Tube, but for London as a whole.

Pick had an anti-Victorian sense of design and was looking for a font that would 'belong unmistakably to the times in which we lived'. He considered using the classical Trajan-style lettering that Eric Gill had created for shopfronts for WH Smith, but judged them too flat; besides, there were already many WH Smith bookstalls on station platforms, and a duplication could be confusing. Pick declared that he wanted something 'straightforward and manly', with each letter in the alphabet 'a strong and unmistakable symbol'.

When Johnston met up again with Pick, and the design was commissioned, he was accompanied by Eric Gill, who helped with Johnston's alphabet before withdrawing because of other work demands (he received 10 per cent of the commissioning fee). Johnston produced his first letters at the end of 1915 – 2-inch capitals of **B**, **D**, **E**, **N**, **O** and **U** – which initially had small serifs. In the lower case the key letter was the o, whose counter (the internal white space) he created equal to twice its stem width, thus giving it 'ideal mass-and-clearance'. His most distinctive letter was the lower-case **L**, which had an upturned boot to distinguish it from I or l. The most beautiful was the i, on which Johnston placed a diamond-shaped dot that still brings a smile today.

The full block-letter alphabet first appeared in 1916. Its creation seems to have been a relatively painless process, with Johnston offering only very few drafts (a confidence born of calligraphic experience). His principal tenet was a search for excellence: 'The letters of the alphabet have certain essential forms,' he wrote when he began the project. 'We have as much right to use the best letters in writing or printing a book as to use the best bricks, if we can get them, in building a house.'

Three of the classic letters from Johnston's alphabet

One of Johnston Sans' earliest appearances was in a draft poster (never issued) advocating the Tube as the safest form of wartime transport:

OUR TRAINS ARE RUN BY LIGHTNING
OUR TUBE LIKE THUNDER SOUND
BUT YOU CAN DODGE THE THUNDERBOLT
BY GOING UNDERGROUND.

And then, handwritten beneath it: *Travel by the bomb-proof Railway!*

The font made its first official appearance in 1916 on a series of workmanlike posters announcing fares from Hammersmith to Twickenham (4d), and promoting the Arts & Crafts Exhibition at the Royal Academy (nearest tube Dover Street, long since closed). Its future use would be more colourful and imaginative, and consistently beautiful:

SEE THE SHOW OF DAHLIAS NEAR
QUEEN ANNE'S GATE

THE FILM-LOVER TRAVELS UNDERGROUND

IN THE COOL OF THE EVENING SEEK OUT
A FRESH AND AIRY SPACE FOR PLEASURE BY
LONDON'S UNDERGROUND

Accompanied by fine prints by Graham Sutherland, Edward Bawden, Paul Nash and Sybil Andrews, the text and artwork promoted London's treasures as never before. It wasn't just promotional material for a transport system — it was a celebration of heritage and cultural well-being. It was also scintillating propaganda: every open-air space, every child-marauding park, would be an unadulterated relief after the overcrowded sooty dankness of the Tube.

Johnston's letters were drawn on tracing paper and then cut in wood, but it is unlikely that he ever envisaged their use much beyond posters and information display, and certainly not as an enduring typeface. Looking back on his work in 1935, he expressed regret that he was more honoured abroad than at home. 'This particular design appears to have become of considerable historic importance (in the world of Alphabets). It seems also to have made a great impression in parts of Central Europe — where I understand it has given

Smoothing out the Johnston roundel

me a reputation which my own country is too practical to recognize.' By the time he died in 1944 this was slowly beginning to change. These days his achievement is widely acknowledged as one of the most successful corporate identities ever created.

As so often with type design, Johnston's font underwent piecemeal adaptations over the years, not all of them happy. After the war, a thinner form, Johnston Light, was used on illuminated boards. Then in 1973, Berthold Wolpe drew a warmer condensed italic to sit alongside Johnston, and the designer Walter Tracy modified some letters – widening the a, lightening the g and, controversially, shortening the tail of the l. But by the end of the 1970s, London Transport's publicity and marketing people were frustrated with the straitjacket of a type designed during the Great War, in a pre-digital age. It lacked variety of weight, it didn't adapt well to new design and printing methods, and increasingly they were tempted by Gill Sans, Univers and a Bembo italic to meet their needs.

Enter Eiichi Kono, a Japanese optics expert who had been studying in London for five years. Working for the British firm Banks & Miles, he was given the daunting task of overhauling Johnston's font. He arrived for his first day at his new job, in 1979, to be confronted by large sheets of the original wood-printed design. 'It felt like my first arrival at London Heathrow Airport,' he recalled, 'worrying about which way to go.' Before he imported a concave lens, microscope and camera from Tokyo, Kono used primitive tools to draft the new letters: black paper, a scalpel, a fine Rotring pen, masking tape, 3M Spray Mount and tweezers.

The original Johnston Sans had only two weights, a regular and a bold. In time, Kono would design eight new ones – including a lighter face and a bolder lower case. He made several alterations to familiar shapes, shortening a few terminals and narrowing the counters within h, m, n and u. He acknowledged two dangers: that he would lose the circular flow of Johnston's original, and that he would end up making a poor clone of Univers. The battle won, Kono found a good way to signal his East Asian input on a London landmark: when he came to present his work for the first time he displayed his various New Johnston fonts with just one word: **Underglound.**

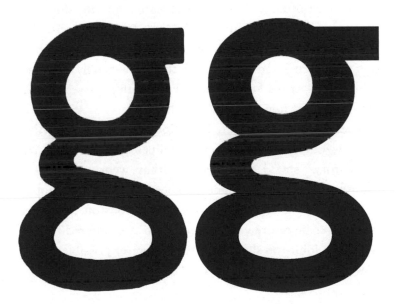

'Old' and 'New' Johnston

Working alongside Kono, Colin Banks was struck by how exceptional it was that an amateur's type had endured for so long. Banks regarded the original Johnston font as 'the most revolutionary and inspirational of twentieth-century letterforms', and there was a reason for this: Johnston still thought with his quill. He was a brilliant primitive, making all his letters the same width and dismissing the accepted rules about 'correct' spacing.

In 1916, the same year that Johnston's work appeared, Lucien Alphonse Legros and John Cameron Grant published their exhaustive study of the optical adjustments that were required of a typeface to aid readability and achieve visually balanced characters (this was the study that observed that a lower-case t often has to lean backwards, and the dot over the i has to be offset a little to the left). Perhaps this is why Johnston's letters still look so radical: they stick out, they don't conform, and they arrest the eye – partly because Johnston never read the manual. Even with the tweaks over the years, their nonconformity endures.

The new types perfected by Kono at Banks & Miles were accompanied by strict guidelines. 'These rules are mandatory,' stated the literature that went to London Transport's in-house designers. 'There must be no attempts to modify them in any way. The New Johnston typefaces must never be re-drawn, re-proportioned or altered in any way. New Johnston should be used wherever possible. If for practical reasons it can't be, use Gill Sans.'

Sixty years after Johnston standardized subterranean London, many of the world's other subway systems remained

Guimard's quintessentially Parisian Métro sign

an uncoordinated scramble; it was a wonder that anyone ever found their connections, or re-emerged into the light.

The Paris Métro was a stunningly confusing place, albeit an enchanting one with all that art nouveau enamel, tiling and metalwork. When it opened for business in 1900, its signage, designed by Hector Guimard, was an elaborate, proud series of curls and swellings that could only be French. As the century advanced, and the network fanned out to the suburbs, each station architect seemed to be given free rein to choose the lettering style they found most pleasing at the time; the local signage would fit the look of Pont de Neuilly or Père Lachaise, but there was no attempt at uniformity.

Things got a little clearer for Parisians in the early 1970s, when Adrian Frutiger was brought in to establish not only some form of unity but also a system versed in legibility. Alphabet Metro was a new form of his Univers, and was all-caps white-on-blue. It was introduced with unusual

The new face of the Paris Métro – Parisine by Jean François Porchez

sensitivity. 'The Métro is like an old lady,' Frutiger declared. 'You can't simply transform her into a modern creature.' Accordingly, new signs were mainly introduced only when old ones broke.

A more complete transformation occurred in the mid-1990s, when Jean François Porchez introduced his font family **Parisine**, a modern and flexible combination of upper and lower case that remains the standard lettering today.

There was a similar story in New York. As it developed, the subway acquired an alluring mess of enamel signs and mosaic tiles in a bewildering range of type – usually a form of Franklin Gothic or Bookman, sometimes with a touch of art deco, occasionally with old-style roman serifs. The jumble was usually attributed to the fact that the subway was an amalgam of three separate train companies – though

Vignelli Associates 1966 designs for the New York City Transit Authority

London's own Tube had six separately managed lines before being integrated as London Transport in 1933.

It was 1967 before the New York subway authorities agreed a grand scheme for establishing uniform station signage. When they did, the typeface chosen was **Standard Medium** (also known as Akzidenz Grotesk), a bold, honest German sans serif from the end of the nineteenth century. It should have worked but adherence to the new system was patchy – many old signs were not removed, while frequently the most dominant signage seemed to be the graffiti that had smothered the subway in the early days of hip hop. In 1979 the *New York Times* reported that 'in many stations the signs are so confusing that one is tempted to wish they were not there at all – a wish that is, in fact, granted in numerous other stations and on all too many of the subway cars themselves.'

But help was at hand. One particular modern font had been proposed for the subway since the mid-1960s, not long after it became widely available in the US. It would appear on the redesigned subway map in 1972, and then in 1989 it was introduced in a medium weight to unify the entire network. As above, so below: subterranean New York had finally succumbed to Helvetica.

What is it about the Swiss?

O r, to be precise: what is it about the Swiss and their sans serif typefaces? Helvetica and Univers both emerged from Switzerland in the same year – 1957 – and went out to shape the modern world. They would sort out not just transport systems but whole cities, and no typefaces ever looked more sure of themselves or their purpose. The two fonts appeared at a time when Europe had thrown off all shackles of post-war austerity and had already made a strong contribution to mid-century modernism. You could sit in your Bertoia Diamond chair (Italy, 1952) and read about a forthcoming concept called IKEA (Sweden, 1958), while all around you buildings began to get squarer and more functional. Helvetica and Univers were perfectly suited

New York's subway goes Helvetica

to this period, and their use reflected another pervasive force of the age – the coming of mass travel and modern consumerism.

Helvetica is a font of such practicality – and, its adherents would suggest, such beauty – that it is both ubiquitous and something of a cult. The typeface even inspired a compelling and successful movie (Gary Hustwit's *Helvetica*), whose premise is that on the streets of the world, the font is like oxygen. You have little choice but to breathe it in.

A few years ago, a New Yorker called Cyrus Highsmith put his life on the line by trying to spend a day without Helvetica. As a type designer himself, he knew it would be a challenge. Whenever he saw something spelled out in the typeface he would have to avert his eyes. He wouldn't take any Helvetica-signed transport, nor buy any Helvetica-branded products. He might have to walk into New York City from its suburbs; possibly go hungry all day.

His troubles began as soon as he climbed out of bed. Most of his clothes had washing instructions in Helvetica, and he struggled to find something that didn't; he settled, eventually, on an old T-shirt and army fatigues. For breakfast he had Japanese tea and some fruit, foregoing his usual yoghurt (Helvetica label). He couldn't read the *New York Times* as that had Helvetica in its tables. The subway was out of the question, though to his relief he found a Helvetica-free bus.

At lunch he thought he'd try Chinatown but had to switch restaurants as the first had a familiar-looking menu. At work he had, in advance, deleted Helvetica from his computer, but he couldn't – obviously – browse the Internet. He was late back home because he couldn't consult the timetable, and had to be highly selective about his cash, as Helvetica graces the new US dollar bills. Inevitably, there was Helvetica on his credit cards, too. In the evening he thought he'd watch TV but the controls had Helvetica on them. So he read *The Long Goodbye* by Raymond Chandler, set in Electra.

After he undertook his non-Helvetica day, Highsmith posed himself a philosophical question. 'Do you need type to live?' The answer of course is no, not in the way one needs food and water. But do you need Helvetica to conduct contemporary urban activity? That's harder to answer.

Gary Hustwit's *Helvetica* movie would suggest you do. His film examines how the font took over the world, opening with shots of the font in Manhattan – on the Times Square tkts booth, Bloomingdale's, Gap, Knoll, the subway, mail-boxes. Then come images of BMW, Jeep, Toyota, Kawasaki, Panasonic, Urban Outfitters, Nestlé, Verizon, Lufthansa, Saab, Oral B, The North Face, Energizer, on and on. The film also tracks the font's genesis, talking to its key surviving creators, none of whom could really comprehend how such a clean little alphabet got so big.

The best section in the movie occurs a third of the way through. The designer Michael Bierut is explaining why Helvetica had such a deep impact on advertising and corporate branding in the 1960s, imagining how remarkable it must have been for an identity consultant to have taken a traditional company like Amalgamated Widget, which was previously represented on its letterheads by a goofy script typeface and a line-drawing of a factory belching smoke, and then sweeping it all away in favour of just one word in Helvetica: Widgco. 'Can you imagine how bracing and thrilling that was?' Bierut asks. 'That must have felt like you had crawled through a desert with your mouth caked with filthy dust, and then someone offers you a clear, refreshing distilled icy glass of water ... it must have just been fantastic.'

Bierut then demonstrates his thoughts by flicking through two contrasting adverts for Coca-Cola, one before Helvetica, and one after. The first one features a smiling family and curly cursive lettering. The second one only shows a big glass of Coke and ice, with vapour bubbles on the glass. The slogan beneath it reads 'It's the real thing. Coke.' Or as Bierut puts it, 'It's the real thing, period. Coke, period. In Helvetica, period. Any questions? Of course not – Drink Coke! Period.'

Helvetica makeover: 'Can you imagine how bracing and thrilling that was?'

Helvetica began life in 1957 as Neue Haas Grotesk, a comprehensive modernization of Akzidenz Grotesk from 1898. It was conceived by Eduard Hoffmann and executed by Max Miedinger for the Haas foundry in Münchenstein, near Basel, and renamed Helvetica (an amended form of Helvetia, the Latin name for Switzerland) in 1960. It was licensed to other, larger, foundries, Stempel of Frankfurt and then Mergenthaler Linotype, and from the mid-1960s it began to gain a reputation overseas, particularly among the design executives on Madison Avenue. The range of weights was restricted initially to light and medium, but when italic, bold and others were added, the face we recognize today began to colonize the world.

It shows no sign of abating. In the spring of 2010, the big in-store push at the troubled clothing manufacturer American Apparel was for the Unisex Viscose Sexuali Tank, available in dark orchid for $24. This is basically a long vest, with all its sizing and washing details displayed – in Helvetica, of course. American Apparel, which uses more Helvetica per square metre than any other place on earth, had realized a simple truth: it doesn't need guile or tricksy emotional psychology to sell its wares – not when it has a bold typeface from Europe that came in with our mother's milk.

Lars Müller, a Norwegian designer who wrote a book about the font, has called Helvetica 'the perfume of the city', while Massimo Vignelli, who first advocated its use on the New York Subway in the 1960s (more than twenty years before it happened), believes its versatility enables the user to say I Love You in a variety of ways, 'with Helvetica Extra

Light if you want to be really fancy ... with the **Extra Bold** if it's really intensive and passionate'. And its appeal is global. In Brussels it is employed throughout the city's transport system. In London the National Theatre has adopted it too, so comprehensively – on its posters, programmes, advertising and signs – that it rivals Johnston's Underground as London's strongest corporate presence.

Only Paris seemed (slightly) resistant to Helvetica's charms. One can find it everywhere on the streets, but an attempt to introduce it underground was less successful. In the Métro it was tried out in the time between Alphabet Metro and Parisine, but in a mish-mash of styles, combining several old and new weights, and it wasn't popular. The problem with Helvetica in a city notably immune to a uniformity of type was that it just wasn't French.

To say Helvetica is 'ubiquitous' is almost like saying cars are everywhere these days. The better observation is that it is ubiquitous because it fulfils so many demands for modern type. So what is it that sets Helvetica apart?

On an emotional plane it serves several functions. It has geographical baggage, its Swiss heritage laying a backdrop of impartiality, neutrality and freshness (it helps at this point if you think of Switzerland as a place of Alps/cow bells/spring flowers rather than Zurich and its erstwhile heroin problem). The font also manages to convey honesty and invite trust, while its quirks distinguish it from anything that portrays overbearing authority; even in corporate use it maintains a friendly homeliness. It wasn't designed with these intentions – it was intended merely as a clean, useful alphabet, and something that would portray important information in the clearest fashion. It wasn't meant for Crate&Barrel homewares store (where it appears with narrow spacing); it was meant for ICI's Schools Liaison Section poster of the periodic table (where it appears in the perfect bold display of upper and lower case – Pd for palladium and Hg for mercury).

On the technical level it looks as if it was designed with some wit, and certainly with the human hand. Like other Swiss designs, it appears that the inner white shapes serve as a firm guide to the black around them, an aspect that one designer called 'a locked-in rightness'.* The majority of its distinguishing features are in lower case: a has a slightly pregnant teardrop belly and a tail; b, d, g, m, n, p, q, r and u have much smaller tails, but they still demand attention in a sans serif face; c, e and s each have straight horizontal endings; the i and j have square dots. On the upper deck, the G has both a horizontal and vertical bar at a right-angle, Q has a short straight angled cross-line like a cigarette in an ashtray, and R has a little kicker for its right leg.

In the 1980s, Linotype rationalized all the disparate Helvetica faces (the old metal types, the short-lived phototypesetting fonts and the digital versions) into one large new family, which it called Helvetica Neue. This is predominantly the type we see everywhere today, although in some cases we may not recognize it as being related to

---

* This was Mike Parker, the man who should be credited with the great expansion of Helvetica in the United States. Parker joined Mergenthaler Linotype in 1959 as design director and immediately began looking for a new adaptable European font that would work at many weights. He oversaw amendments to the Swiss designs to suit the hot metal process, and realized he had hit a goldmine.

the original font, such is the range of weights. There are fifty-one different styles to choose from at Linotype. com, including some that hardly look like the original at all: Helvetica Neue Ultra Light Italic, *H N Condensed Ultra Light Oblique,* HN Bold Outline.

In Bloomsbury, in the shadow of the British Museum, the office of Simon Learman is covered in Helvetica. Learman is joint executive creative director at McCann Erickson, and since he took up this post in 2006 he has been involved in campaigns for American Airlines, the only airline not to have changed its core typeface in more than forty years. It is, of course, in Helvetica, usually in red (American) and blue (Airlines). For a while, PanAm used Helvetica too, but one now associates the font instantly with its one-time rival.

On one wall of Learman's office there are a number of showcards with his recent hits. His work for Heinz Salad Cream uses a type that is also rooted in the 1950s, but slightly washed out, linking it with endless summers and post-war austerity. Next to it, Heinz Big Soup is sold with a bloated font, full of its own cud-chewing goodness. These are specialist types carefully sourced from the online directories. But next to them are bold Helvetica capitals offering 'SOLITARY REFINEMENT' above a photograph of a wide leather seat, and 'THE RED THE WHITE AND THE BLUE' above a photo of two bottles of wine and a window on a cloudless sky. These are newspaper adverts, and have an unusually large amount of text, chiselled in the shape of skyscrapers. 'Ahhh ... Blissful solitude', the first of these ads begins. 'Imagine floating high above the earth cocooned in your own perfect little world ...' The seduction – about ergonomically designed pods and a highly indulgent cabin crew, and lots of puns about 'a long stretch' – goes on for quite a while, and beneath it, in bold italics, are the facts: how many flights a day, the many gateway cities and the website address.

Helvetica has familiarity on its side, but it is also still inherently useful in selling a tiring day of travel. 'The thinking was,' Simon Learman says, 'that it has to compete against the British Airways brand, which is majestic "Britain at its best", and Virgin, which is "rock'n'roll and rock star lifestyle". So with this campaign we tried to evoke what travel used to be like. The luxury of the 1950s, early 60s, a little bit *Mad Men*. The American Airlines position was that they flew more New Yorkers than anyone else, so by dint of the fact that New Yorkers are difficult … if we can keep New Yorkers happy then we can keep you happy.' Helvetica has come to represent getting things done efficiently. 'It's about getting to your meeting on time and getting the deal, but it's also about using the type to be very businesslike in the way the ad talks to you.'

Learman gets out some other cards from a cupboard, a campaign that didn't run. 'This is one of those heartbreakers,' he says. Here, the type itself is the message: on one advert the A extending itself until it turns into a long seat, on another two As forming themselves into the legs of a trestle table

AmericanAirlines®

Helvetica might not rock but it has a message

to emphasize the amount of working space on a business flight. 'American really liked the idea, but they were nervous that it may invite people to start playing with their logo and damage their reputation.'

In 1957, when Helvetica still had its old name and was yet to make its mark on the world, the French type foundry Deberny & Peignot announced what it hoped would be a new and revolutionary font: Univers. Called upon to explain the name, its Swiss-born designer Adrian Frutiger explained that it was almost called Galaxy and then Universal. But Univers was the perfect aggrandizing title for a font designed to replace the fading Futura as the ultimate symbol of a new Europe, for a font that could lay claim to being THE BEST TYPEFACE IN THE WORLD. It is still a wonderful thing. Univers doesn't age or sag, and everything you say with it will have a ring of authority.

Frutiger, born in the picturesque Swiss Oberland in 1928, is one of the great type theorists. He asserts that type has the power 'to make the whole world of thought legible simply by re-arranging the same letters over and over again', and Univers was his first great vehicle. In 1957 Deberny & Peignot launched it with a Madison Avenue-style slogan: 'Univers: a synthesis of Swiss thoroughness, French elegance and British precision in pattern manufacture.' The phrase gives itself away in its vocabulary: most type designers before Univers thought they were making an alphabet; but in the emerging age of phototypesetting it is the pattern that is all the rage.

The font had a long and painstaking gestation. In 1952, Frutiger was headhunted by D&P to develop new fonts for its Lumitype system, a novel phototypesetting machine that stored the impressions of a keyboard as binary figures in a computer memory bank. In many ways a forerunner to the desktop computer, it speeded composition, achieved new levels of accuracy, and extended the options of the designer. The process did not become as successful as its rivals but it led to some wonderful fonts. The machine required that each typeface appear on a separate interchangeable disk, and so Frutiger, then only twenty-four but already gaining a reputation as a leading young designer in Switzerland, took the train to France and started work.

Not long after his arrival, he rushed out a few minor works: PRESIDENT and Ondine, the former a POINTED SLIGHTLY GOTHIC SERIF, the latter a thick-nibbed calligraphic font with Arabic overtones. But then, over a period of four years, Frutiger created Univers, a font that chimed perfectly with what we understand to be the pinnacle of cool European modernism – sans serif, inspiration from Roman capitals, a smoothness and harmony, a uniformity of height both in capitals and lower case, and horizontally cut curved ends (known as 'finals', a trait that Univers shares with Helvetica, most noticeable on the C and S; earlier san serifs had diagonal cuts).

The British type designer Stanley Morison, originator of Times New Roman, called Univers 'the least bad' sans serif face, while others disapproved of its slightly chilly quality. Some objected to a 'mistake' on the lower-case g, with the ending of its open tail being too close to the bowl. But if you wanted to go somewhere in safety in the new Europe of the 1950s, then Univers was for you.

Adrian Frutiger (seated) checking his Univers

There is a telling photograph of Frutiger in a large light room in Paris looking at a big board of his Univers letters. He sits on a stool with his back to the camera while a man in a white labcoat stands besides the board, seemingly waiting instructions. It is like an eye examination, but one where the patient is so relaxed that he has stopped looking at the A and B, and is looking at the space that surrounds them separately and jointly, and the qualities that link those letters to an M or an S or a V.

The photo marks the point when the design of type moved from something performed primarily with the eye through the hand, to something that resulted from science. Virtuosity and beauty were no longer the things. Now there was a calibrated measuring chart on which visibility and legibility would be tracked with precision. Men in labcoats and clipboards were now defining our alphabet – a long way from Gutenberg, Caslon or Baskerville.

Once it was scientifically proven, Frutiger demonstrated his creation by using the word Monde, hinting at great ambitions. His font appeared on signs and instructions and advertising, the whole family spanning a vast range of twenty-one weights, from Extra Light Condensed to **Extra Black Extended**, its availability extending far beyond Lumitype to the traditional hot-metal casting of Monotype and Linotype machines, an expansion requiring the carving of 35,000 individual punches.

Univers made public appearances across Europe over the next half century, notably in London, where Westminster adopted **UNIVERS BOLD CONDENSED** for its street signs; Munich, which chose it as the face of its 1972 Olympics; and Paris, where, being at least part French, it was a natural for the updating of the Métro. The choice was later echoed by the Montréal Métro and the San Francisco BART.

Zeitplan
Calendrier
Schedule
26.8.–10.9.1972

	Sa Sa Sa 26.	So Di Su 27.	Mo Lu Mo 28.	Di Ma Tu 29.	Mi Me We 30.	Do Je Th 31.	Fr Ve Fr 1.	Sa Sa Sa 2.	So Di Su 3.	Mo Lu Mo 4.	Di Ma Tu 5.	Mi Me We 6.	Do Je Th 7.	Fr Ve Fr 8.	Sa Sa Sa 9.	So Di Su 10.
Leichtathletik / Athlétisme / Track and Field																
Rudern / Aviron / Rowing																
Basketball / Basketball / Basketball																
Boxen / Boxe / Boxing																
Kanu / Canoë / Canoeing																
Radfahren / Cyclisme / Cycling																
Fechten / Escrime / Fencing																

The schedule of events from the 1972 Munich Olympics

The font remains in wide use and its clarity has found a lasting role on Rand McNally and Ordnance Survey maps, at General Electric and Deutsche Bank – and on Apple's keyboards (until they turned to VAG Rounded in 2007). But, despite being regarded by many as superior to Helvetica in legibility and contrast, it has not achieved Helvetica's lasting fame and superstar status. It is not the subject of T-shirts or documentary films.

Frutiger himself blames the font's (relative) decline on production methods: Univers achieved its finest results in its original hot metal, while the adaptations to more modern photo- and laser-setting systems were inexactly realized. But there are other reasons – notably the snowballing effect of public taste. Like no font before or after it, Helvetica achieved a tipping point, and it shows no sign of waning. Wherever you go, there it is.

Frutiger

Mention your admiration of Univers – or even Helvetica – to a font enthusiast and they are quite likely to respond by talking about Frutiger. Frutiger is the typeface that many typographers believe is the finest ever made for signs and directions. And the reason Frutiger is better than Adrian Frutiger's previous exceptional sans serif, Univers? Because Univers, although a milestone in font design, can be a little rigid and strict: a Univers lower-case e, for example, is almost a circle with a cut in it, both precise and scary. Whereas Frutiger is perfect.

Frutiger was just twenty eight when he designed Univers, and it displays signs of being an intellectual exercise. By the time he created Frutiger, he was in his fifties, surer of his place in the world, his hand more relaxed. His new font had a more humane feel, with a few details that have no mathematical logic, but just please the eye. Considering its predominant use on information boards, it is unusually warm and welcoming.

The font was designed for Roissy Airport in the early 1970s, before its renaming as Paris Charles de Gaulle. It had to look clear and concise on illuminated boards and signs with yellow backgrounds, and it began life with Frutiger cutting out black paper to make the words **Départs** and **Departures**. Particular

Roissy Airport – the original terminus for Frutigerland

attention was given to the need to read words at an angle, and to calculations of size: a letter ten centimetres high was required to be legible at twenty metres. The Frutiger arrow was forceful but squat, almost square. He viewed the whole project as creating 'an arrivals and departure machine'.

Frutiger was all for aesthetics in his work, but something else was paramount. 'If you remember the shape of your spoon at lunch, it has to be the wrong shape,' he told his admirers at a type conference in 1990. 'The spoon and the letter are tools; one to take food from the bowl, the other to take information off the page ... When it is a good design, the reader has to feel comfortable because the letter is both banal and beautiful.'

Like Helvetica and Univers, Frutiger is getting dangerously hard to avoid. It has become a standard information bearer at many large institutions, especially universities. It has evolved into a large family, with a serif version and many weights and italics, and Frutiger Stones offering thick playful letters within an irregular pebble shape just begging to be made into fizzy sweets. And it has come to the aid of sports commentators.

Square-shouldered American football players usually trot onto the field with Collegiate or Varsity on their backs – rectangular and chunky fonts matching their physiques. But Europeans seldom appear in their national type. The Germans wouldn't be seen in 𝕱𝖗𝖆𝖐𝖙𝖚𝖗 or Futura, but commonly wear **Serpentine** (American), while the French are just as happy with Optima (German) as with Peignot. The Portuguese and Brazilians have scored with something close to **Univers** (Swiss), while the Argentinians have tackled **ITC Bauhaus** (America out of Germany). The England football team have appeared with **Gill Sans** between their shoulders, although they've settled in recent years on something approaching **Antique Olive**, which is French. Perhaps they should give **Comic Sans** a run.

These fonts tend not to be the choice of the midfield general, but of Adidas, Nike or Umbro, who will buy a famous type and tweak it to make it theirs. In the 2010 World Cup in South Africa, the winners, Spain, wore Unity, created by Yomar Augusto for

Antique Olive, Univers and ITC Bauhaus – not a bad strike force

Adidas. But increasingly the default setting in the domestic leagues has been **Arial Black** or **Frutiger**, the easiest way to read a name from the back of the east stand upper.

A similar uniformity has tempered European travel. Frutiger could almost be called World Airport, such is its growing influence and acceptance. In 2000 you would land at Heathrow, and the signs to passport control would be in a very British customized **Bembo**, with grand serifs. That alone was enough to confirm you had landed in the right place. Fly into Heathrow today and you will be in **Frutigerland**, or a lightly customized form of it. The United States has so far resisted its charms, hanging on to Helvetica, but most of Europe has adopted it.

But a default can be a good thing, especially if it gets your luggage back.

10

Road
Akzidenz

At the time when Switzerland was giving birth to Helvetica and Univers, an Englishman called Jock Kinneir and a South African woman, Margaret Calvert, were creating a parallel revolution in Britain. If you do any driving in Europe, in Britain or Ireland, Spain or Portugal, Denmark or Iceland, you will be entirely familiar with their work. For it is their lettering, **Transport**, that is used on almost all of these countries' motorway signs. It appears, too, in places as far afield as China and Egypt and Dubai, for signs with English translations. And Kinneir and Calvert did something else important: they established that it is a lot easier to read lower-case letters than capitals when travelling at speed.

Calvert was born in Durban in 1936, and one of the first things she remembers after arriving in Britain as a teenager is being taken to London's South Bank to see the Festival of Britain, a symbol of the future. She now lives in Islington, north London, a nice quiet townhouse if it wasn't for the fact that visitors are continually reminded of children crossing, and men at work, and the possibility of cows becoming part of the proceedings at any time. Triangular warning traffic signs are littered around her front room and in the hallway. The girl taking the boy by the hand? That was Calvert's memory of herself as a schoolgirl. The pictogram of a man digging earth to indicate roadworks (or struggling to open an umbrella, in popular mythology)? That was Calvert's work, too. 'The people in charge now have messed things

Margaret Calvert at home with her road signs

up,' she says, as she shows me the differences between her original children and the digital ones we have now.

Calvert fell into her career by accident. She was at Chelsea School of Art, not quite deciding between painting and illustration, when a visiting lecturer noticed her diligence. This was Jock Kinneir, a well-regarded designer who had just set up his own business. Calvert had enjoyed some of his previous assignments in class, not least the task of designing a new promotional leaflet for the Battersea Fun Fair. The fair, a rather tawdry offshoot from its elegant birth as the Battersea Pleasure Gardens in 1951, offered the Big Dipper and the Wheel of Death, and a place to make your own spin paintings. It had changed a bit since it opened as part of the Festival of Britain, but it was still an exciting and popular attraction (at least until children started dying on its rides), and its fantasies were mostly those of speed and space. It was a place where a young artist could express her creativity.

Impressed with Calvert's work as a student, in 1957 Kinneir asked her to help him with a larger project with similar themes: the signs at the new Gatwick Airport. Kinneir's own experience of this kind of thing was related to designing the pavilions at the Festival of Britain and exhibition stands at Wembley. He hadn't applied for the job – he got it after chatting to one of Gatwick's architects, David Allford, at a Green Line bus stop on their way to work. Still, how hard could it be to design a panel saying 'Departures'?

In his initial report, Kinneir listed a few typefaces that might work, among them Gill Sans. But none proved ideal, so he started from scratch, much influenced by Edward Johnston's letters for the London Underground. Calvert remembers the end result as 'a rather inelegant but nevertheless very clear' hybrid between Johnston and Monotype Grotesque 216.

The opening of the airport was a success, and few paid much attention to the appearance of the signs, which is as it should be (the directions were printed white on green). But one person who did notice them was Colin Anderson, the chairman of P&O Orient. He asked Kinneir to design the luggage labels for passengers taking his cruise ships. 'If you get noticed for signs,' Calvert says, 'that's what you become. The work just snowballed. The labels were designed specifically for illiterate porters, making it easy for them to identify baggage by colour and shape.'

But it was Colin Anderson's next job that made Kinneir and Calvert famous. In 1957, Anderson was appointed chairman of the committee to advise on motorway road signs. The first stage of what was to become the M1, between London and Yorkshire, was under construction, and there was a lot of new information to display at speed. Anderson's committee appointed Kinneir as their design consultant.

He and Calvert were offered a little guidance: 'I am anxious you shouldn't embark upon inventing an alphabet of a character quite "new",' Anderson wrote in a letter in June 1958. 'We have as a committee got into the habit of accepting the general weight and appearance of the German alphabet as being the sort of thing we need.'

'It was a request which we chose to ignore,' Calvert remembers. The German alphabet referred to was DIN (Deutsche Industrie Norm), the plainest of faces used for autobahns and West German number plates. It was developed in the 1920s, with strokes of even thickness aiding readability. Engineers felt comfortable with it, not least because it bore no trace of artistry and got you where you needed to go. But Kinneir and Calvert believed DIN to be too crude, and thought it would not fit well within the softer English landscape.

They looked at other possibilities, not least another German face called Akzidenz Grotesk, an early sans serif from the end of the nineteenth century. One contemporary designer has described Akzidenz as being 'both approachable and aggressive at the same time,' which may be just the qualities one demands of a sign: the clear type reads well from a distance but its thin, consistent and rather monotone letters don't detain the imagination long.

In Britain and America, Akzidenz Grotesk was usually called Standard, a suitable name for something with such little personality. It was to become a key inspiration for both Univers and Helvetica, but its main use in the first half of the twentieth century was for trade catalogues and price lists. It is one of the most significant faces without the name of a recognized designer attached, seemingly being designed by committee at the Berthold foundry, before being modernized and enlarged in the 1950s by Günter Gerhard Lange.

Akzidenz Grotesk – 'approachable and aggressive'

The new alphabet developed by Kinneir and Calvert would soon have a name – Transport – and its features would guide drivers all over the world, not least the curve on the end of the l (borrowed from Johnston), and the obliquely cut curved strokes of the letters a, c, e, f, g, j, s, t and y. The letterforms were specifically designed to enable drivers to read place names as swiftly as possible, and the duo had found a simple truth: word recognition was easier and faster when upper and lower case combined. This wasn't just a question of legibility; we seldom read an entire word before comprehending it, and skimming is easier when the letters flow as they do in a book. But the letters were only half the battle; it was their exact use on signs that would be just as challenging.

The pair made numerous presentations to members of the Road Research Laboratory and men from the Department of Transport, and they spoke of such things as the impact of headlights and halation, the light-flooding effect that meant that white-on-black letters should be slightly thinner than black-on-white. They agreed that the signs should be able to display all their information from 600 feet away. They also discussed colour. Calvert remembers a visit by Sir Hugh Casson, the architect considered to be Britain's leading design expert, who suggested the signs should be 'as dark as old dinner jackets'. Instead they drew influence from the United States, settling for white letters on American Standard Interstate Blue.

When the weather permitted, Kinneir and Calvert moved out of their Knightsbridge office and placed their prototype signs in the courtyard outside and against tree trunks in

Hyde Park; and then they walked slowly away from them, establishing relative reading distances. Their signs were tested on the Preston Bypass, and swiftly became as much a part of the landscape as disappearing trees and new Little Chefs. Not long after the first section of the M1 motorway opened in 1959, the big blue slabs of information proved so effective that nobody gave them a second glance.

But soon there would be another major problem to deal with – the signage and typography of Britain's ordinary roads, the subject of another heavyweight Department of Transport committee. This was something that had not been successfully addressed since the Romans scratched Londinium in soft stone pillars.

In July 1961, the typographer Herbert Spencer took a twenty-mile journey from Marble Arch to what was then called London Airport at Heathrow. He took his camera along, and published the results in a lavish essay in his periodical *Typographica*. He wasn't expecting to be impressed by design unity and a perfect choice of type, but he was surprised by the complete chaos of signs he encountered, which he described as 'an extraordinary barrage of prose' confronting drivers with as much text as a novel. The signs were 'prohibitory, mandatory, directional, informative or warning ... a remarkable demonstration of literary and graphic inventiveness in a field where discipline and restraint would be more appropriate and less dangerous.'

Spencer, who would later become a colleague of Margaret Calvert at the Royal College of Art, was a champion of modernity, and an enthusiast for the asymmetrical

The drive-by testing of transport fonts

typography advanced by Jan Tschichold in Munich and the fluency and clarity of sans serif experiments of the Bauhaus. His horror at London's street signs provoked editorials in the *Guardian* and *Times Literary Supplement*, and almost certainly came to the attention of the Worboys Committee, the transport group charged with producing a more user-friendly system. Jock Kinneir was the obvious choice for this work, but his proposals – Transport type again, but now white on green with yellow numerals for A-routes and black on white for B-routes, designed around a strict set of rules based on a tiling system – did not go unopposed.

Another designer, David Kindersley, believed they were muscling in on his patch. Kindersley had been thinking about alphabets and spacing for many years, and had done titling work for the Shell Film Unit. He had produced a more traditional serif alphabet for local road signs that took up less space despite being all capitals. But times were changing: his MOT Serif font was a reassuring companion on the road to Datchet or Windsor, but it didn't look as if it would withstand the increasingly scientific rigours of the road research labs.

The key to Kinneir and Calvert's work was careful letter-spacing on a tiling system without the loss of word-shape. As with the motorway signs, the whole system was designed from the driver's point of view. 'The key is ensuring that one has time to react accordingly,' Calvert explains. 'It's about word recognition rather than requiring a driver to read each letter in a word. Jock would say it was like a Seurat pointillist painting. I always compared it to the Rembrandt portraits in Amsterdam: if you're close up it doesn't make any sense but it all comes together at the appropriate reading distance.' Moreover, the Kinneir/Calvert system combined a universal amalgamation of words, numbers, directions and pictograms, a package closer to satellite navigation displays than it was to Kindersley's beautifully wrought letter theories.

The clash of theories between Kindersley and Kinneir/Calvert turned to open conflict, with angry letters to *The Times*. It increasingly looked as if Kindersley objected not only to the new look but also to being usurped by two relative upstarts. The battle was really between the old world and the new, the serif and the sans. Kindersley was a calligrapher and master stonemason, a pupil of Eric Gill,

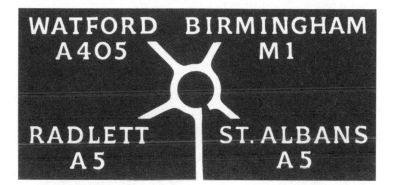

The way it almost looked: David Kindersley's proposed sign lettering (above) and an early version of the lower-case sans serif Kinneir/Calvert design that won the day.

a believer in the ethics of the workshop, a man who liked traditional letter-spacing and exhibited his skill nowhere better than in his carving for the American War Cemetery near Cambridge. What he didn't necessarily like was the Swiss style of clean efficiency that Kinneir and Calvert were both edging towards. There was only one way to solve their conflict: there would be a duel.

A testing area was set up at Benson Airport, the RAF base in Oxfordshire. 'They got several airmen to sit in chairs on a platform,' Calvert remembers, 'and on the top of an old Ford Anglia they'd fixed these test signs with just two destinations on them, and they drove them towards these airmen and they had to say which ones they could see or read first.' Kindersley's was found to be slightly more legible ('Three per cent!' Calvert says. 'A negligible amount!'). But on aesthetic grounds the committee wasn't in any doubt which lettering they preferred.

After Transport, Margaret Calvert worked on a new face for Britain's NHS hospitals, based on Helvetica, which she later adapted for British Rail (British Rail Alphabet) and then all BAA airports. Jock Kinneir died in 1994, David Kindersley the following year. Now in her seventies, Margaret Calvert regrets the encroaching sloppiness and proliferation of present-day signage, although she is pleased that her contribution to the original work is being recognized. 'It's funny how it swings around,' she says. 'It used to be that Jock got all the credit, now it's me. According to some people I've signposted the world, which of course is ridiculous.'

Her name will live on for another reason, too. In the 1970s Kinneir and Calvert had won a competition to design all the graphics and communications for a new town in France, Saint-Quentin-en-Yvelines. Calvert remembers being bored, by this time, with sans serif letterforms such as Gill Sans and Helvetica, and, wanting something with a French feel, she started experimenting with serif fonts.

The face she came up with looked a little like the slab-serif Egyptian fonts from the early nineteenth century, sturdy but full of vitality, but the French rejected it, saying it looked too English. Then it found another use. An entire communications system was required for the Tyne and Wear Metro, and the new slab serif seemed to sit equally well with Newcastle's monumental architectural history. The name Metro was already taken, so when the new face was made available as a digital typeface, Monotype called it **Calvert**. Rather fittingly, it is today resplendent in stainless-steel letters outside the Royal College of Art in South Kensington, not far from the spot where Kinneir and Calvert used to try out the road signs more than fifty years before.

DIY 11

Most of us are type designers from birth. We begin scribbling as toddlers, the most freedom we will ever have. Then we conform to a style, we raise the pen above and below the dotted line, we are rewarded for good copying. In Britain, the classic teachers of how to write, followed by the twentieth century's children and their teachers, were Marion Richardson and Tom Gourdie – the latter, the author of the *Ladybird Book of Handwriting*. 'The writer should be seated comfortably,' Gourdie instructed us all, 'feet flat on the floor and the desk sloping slightly ... The forefinger should rest on the pencil about one-and-a-half inches from the point, and should point into the paper at an angle of 45 degrees.' All sound advice for the child equipped with a 'Black Prince pencil, or Platignum fountain pen with medium nib'.

Gourdie, whose work had an international following, was awarded an MBE in the 1970s, when the biggest enemy of beautiful handwriting was not the computer, but the Biro. 'The ball point pen is most emphatically discouraged,' he wrote. With only minor adjustments, his principles hold firm today. At the very start, Gourdie directs the young hand away from drawing letters, and displays merely strokes, circles and jagged edges. Then there are exercises for the 'clockwise' letters m, n, h, k, b, p and r, followed by the anti-clockwise (all the others). First names were used as a good way of using all the letters together: George, Hugh, Ian, James, Kate. The letters were then joined up, the loops on the bottom of the t and the top of the r

Tom Gourdie demonstrating handwriting principles

found their purpose in tea, toe, rope and ride, which led to the most important exercise of all, the sandwiching of n between pairs of identical letters: ana, bnb, cnc, dnd. The verse Gourdie used to bring everything together in a tender italic at the end was:

One, two, three, four, five
Once I caught a fish alive

And once you had mastered that, it was time to get a John Bull Printing Outfit for your birthday.

The John Bull set – a typographic outlet for kids for forty years from its launch in the 1930s – contained tweezers, rubber letters, a wooden or plastic stamping rack to mount them on, and ink pad and paper. This kit was the fifteenth-century Gutenberg Bible writ small and smudgy – movable type to be used and reused until the tiny letters got lost in the carpet. The sets ranged from the compact unnumbered original to No 155, the larger numbers also containing rubber picture stamps. (The numbers were seemingly chosen at random: there was no No 11, for instance, and the larger numbers didn't necessarily promise a bigger box or better things.)

The instructions for Outfit No 4 explained how to be your own Caxton, and it wasn't complicated. 'Separate the India-rubber type carefully. The letters are merely pressed into the holder. When the word or sentence is complete see that the face of the type is level. To print, carefully ink type on the pad … Should pad dry, damp the surface with a little water.' Was there a child in the land who couldn't grasp these principles? And was there one who didn't use their own name for their very first words?

Careful now, keep it level – the John Bull Printing Outfit, 1950s wooden version

This was a wonderful British product, and not just by name. John Bull – stout, reliable, red-faced – was an emblem of olde stoicism and resistance. If he wasn't on your packet of plump pork sausages he was on your frothing Toby jug, holding the nation up by his britches while the dog by his side looked unstrokable. The Printing Outfit was the perfect inter-war product, supporting both the toy and the rubber industries. The makers of Quink ink did okay from it too, parents loved it because it was educational, and children kept using it because they could construct rude words and secret messages over and over. We were making something, and in any self-respecting middle-class family of the 1960s it was there with the Spirograph as proud objects of reusable creativity.

Just the mention of it may send a grown man to eBay, though few would go to the extreme of artist John Gillett, who mounted a show at the Bracknell Gallery in Berkshire in 2004 called *John Bull War and Peace*, in which he showed a video of him tweezering his way through Tolstoy's classic. Gillett didn't really print the whole book, but he was making a point about how long art takes to make. A few years later, Stephen Fry used Printing Outfit No 30 at the start of his compelling BBC TV film about Gutenberg.

The John Bull kit didn't teach you how to spell, and it didn't tell you much about typefaces, but it was the handling and appreciation of letters that was important, a hands-on introduction to something that could be useful in later life.

More useful but less fun was the American manufactured Dymo label maker, a crunchy piece of plastic everyone could use to put their name on things that might be stolen. The operation took a while, and some strength: you threaded a loop of thin sticky tape onto a stamping plate, lined up a letter in a wheel, and squeezed a lever to emboss it in white. After a few minutes of twisting and pressing and cutting you had a word or two, which you could then put on books and files and LP sleeves. Then there were two possible outcomes: the labels

Dymo – an invention that stuck ... sometimes

would fall off and refuse adhesion thereafter, or they would stick so well that the surface of your possessions would be ruined forever.

Dymo set up business in California in 1958 and somehow the company still exists, although the modern machines have little motors and self-adhesive stickers. The original contraptions offered only one typeface (DYMO ROMAN), with variety introduced by different-coloured tape reels.

The world of personal printing changed completely with Letraset. This was not just a party invitation tool, nor a kid's toy, but a major part of the international graphic design industry. It was also the first time anyone outside the printing industry could choose a favourite font from the comfort of their desk, and the vast choice available introduced new words to common studio usage: Compacta, Pump, Premier Shaded, Octopus Shaded, Stack, Optex, Frankfurter, InterCity and Nice One Cyril. Letraset also created the first wave of 'desktop publishing', before the phrase existed. Letraset headings punctuated most of the punk fanzines and student press of the late 1970s and early 1980s, anticipating by a decade the liberation of computer DTP.

The Letraset company began in London in 1959, and by 1961 its founder Dai Davies had found a way to 'liberate the letter' from the restrictions of the letterpress and phototypesetting industries. No longer would magazine and poster designers, or engineers, schoolteachers and information managers, have to leave their regular place of work, run to the printers with a list of typeface names and

Perfect technique – a Letraset expert at work

empty space on their pages, and wait for a technician to make their headlines. Suddenly they were their own technicians, and they could be up all night rubbing until they ran out of the letter e.

The technique was the Dry Transfer process, which entailed 'burnishing' (ie rubbing) a letter from a tacky sheet of plastic onto the desired surface until you got the whole thing on without creasing, and then repeating the exercise until you had a word that was (almost) straight. With patience it was possible to master this, and the results could be satisfying. The system was frowned upon by the traditional typographic trades, whose workers treated it initially as risible, and then as a threat that wouldn't go away. (Letraset was the dominant force in this hungry market, but it wasn't the first rub-down process. The French got there first, the foundry Deberny & Peignot offering Typophane, sticky letters of their most famous types on a carrier film. But you had to cut out the letters individually before rubbing them, and their edges were often visible. Letraset simplified this process, and had one other great asset: relentless marketing.)

From a distance it is tricky to remember just how transformative Letraset was. It put a self-made lettering artist in every home or office, and it reshaped typography almost as much as hot metal compositing had done sixty-five years before. Its instruction sheet, keen not to be mistaken for something simple, adopted the faintly scientific air of a moon landing: 'Burnish onto surface – the lettering will turn translucent as it is transferred from the carrier sheet.'

Wonky Letraset heading and dodgy typewriter ribbon – a winning combination for punk fanzines and student mags

What remains? Some childhood nostalgia, a fleeting mention in the Arctic Monkeys song 'Cornerstone', and the sporadic reunions of those who thought they had found the future. Twenty years after its heyday in the mid-1970s, a group of stencil cutters from Letraset recalled their experiences for a booklet published by the St Bride Library with the ITC of New York, and their abiding vision was of an eccentric world much missed (at least by them). They recalled making special tools of wood sticks, Sellotape and razor blades to cut sheets of letters out of Ulano masking film, and they explained how difficult this method was, particularly if one wanted to avoid 'the dreaded peanut', a visible link between straight and curved cuts.

The master Letraset cutter would make letters look as though they had been carved with a single stroke. It was a process that could take six weeks for an entire alphabet, before the letters were finally deemed worthy of photographic reproduction and then mass printing on thin plastic sheets. Freda Sack recalled a two-year training period, and then taking two days to cut each letter of her ornate Masquerade. Mike Daines, another professional cutter, remembered an office high on the Beatles and marijuana when he started in 1967, and for years afterwards was unable to enjoy drawing letters in the sand on beach holidays without fearing an admonishing head-shaking from the supervisors.

But Letraset was not only a boon for graphic designers; it was also a wonderful thing for typefaces. Two years from its launch in 1961, the sticky letters were available in 35 standard fonts, while a decade later, marketed to 96 countries, there were 120 standard faces and at least 40 more in the specialized Letragraphica range. The latter was available on subscription only: designers who thought of themselves as cutting edge signed up to receive what Letraset executive Anthony Wenman called typefaces that were 'as hot-off-the-press as one can get'.

The ultimate accolade came when the world's leading traditional type designers, including Hermann and Gudrun Zapf (Palatino, Optima, Zapfino, Diotima, Zapf Dingbats), Herb Lubalin (Eros, Fact), and Aaron Burns (co-founder of the ITC font foundry), came all the way to Letraset headquarters in Ashford, Kent, to pay their respects. They were surprised to find a factory entirely without windows – to ensure dust-free surfaces – where men and women worked with the precision of watchmakers. It was a future in which its participants never got ink on their hands.

The company secured the rights of sixty classic fonts. Helvetica was becoming dominant in the early 1960s, and there were chart placings for Garamond, Times Bold, Futura, Caslon and Plantin. Letraset also employed its own staff to make new fonts, and in 1973 held an International Typeface Design Competition, which attracted 2,500 entries. The prize was £1,000, and seventeen faces were selected for production. They were predominantly based on traditional scripts, and had names like Magnificat and Le Griffe.

Letraset was the dominant force in dry transfer, but others also tried their hand. There was rub-down rivalry from Craft Creations of Cheshunt, who produced sheets with whole words, thus eliminating the nightmare of spacing. Sheet 103 read: *Happy Anniversary Love Anniversary Wishes Anniversary Congratulations Engagement* ... ' – all in flowery *Harlequin*, the elaborate capitals as wispy as horse hair swatting flies. 'Results will vary with technique,' a guide sheet explained with nerveless understatement. 'Remember, practice makes perfect.'

If people outside of the design world knew the name of any fonts before Letraset arrived, they probably worked in an office and were female. The IBM Selectric Typewriter first appeared in 1961, and changed the look not only of professional documents, but also of professional desks. The machine's keyboard didn't look like an old Remington or Olivetti; in fact, its integral sunken keys looked uncannily like those on a laptop. And the results were similar, too. If you had the inspiration and vast amounts of patience you could write the first line of a sales order in Prestige Pica 72, the second in Orator or Delegate, and the rest of the thing in Courier 12 Italic.

The trick was the Golfball or Typeball, the interchangeable rounded metal sphere that you could click in and out of the centre console and get less ink on your hands than from changing a ribbon. IBM had twenty different golfball typefaces for sale, most of them sober and undramatic, but different enough to usher in the concept of corporate branding for even the smallest of businesses. IBM called its balls not fonts but 'typing elements', and its users' manual confidently asserted that 'you'll find one right for every typing job'. It wasn't the first to offer a choice of types – that claim lay with the portable Blickensderfer typewriter

The IBM Selectric's secret weapon – its inner golfball
(about the size of a £2 coin)

from the 1890s. But the Selectric was the first to make the switching of fonts a relatively easy option. At its peak in the 1980s, the Selectric dominated the global professional marketplace. But type always evolves. Once you could snap in a ball, or stamp, cut, emboss and rub, there was only one further thing to master: turning on Your First Computer.

Even in its most basic, green-screen, fish-memory, floppy disk state – let's say a bottom of the range Amstrad PCW – this would rapidly make everything else to do with type obsolete. Once you could use a computer keyboard and press the print button, why expect a future for a Platignum or Golfball? Once you had a calculator, what on earth was all that fuss about multiplication tables? Once you had email, why would you need a Post Office clerk to stick strips of type on a telegram? And once you had digital music, too bad for burnished sleevenotes. Hand-printing, Letraset – they didn't stand a chance. And calligraphy is virtually gone, a craft Prince Charles is said to be keen on, hanging on grimly behind glass on the qualification certificates of quantity surveyors and chiropractors.

Now, almost everything we need is to be found beneath an LED or plasma screen. The tension of graphite or nib, or the fragile pleasure to be derived from running a forefinger across the opening page of a well-printed book, is fast becoming heritage. But typefaces – both their preponderance and ingenuity – have not suffered a similar decline in fortunes. Quite the opposite: it is now their almost inestimable number that is proving problematic.

What the Font?

When it was first published, in 1953, the *Encyclopaedia of Type Faces* caused waves of shock and delight in the design world. The shock, and the delight, was that there were so many typefaces in it – hundreds upon hundreds, from Achtung to Zilver Type. The book was edited by W Turner Berry (Librarian at St Bride Printing Library) and AF Johnson (Keeper of Books at the British Museum), joined for the next edition by writer and publisher W Pincus Jaspert, and offered a valuable opportunity to survey five hundred years of type history. As successive editions appeared, the featured fonts were accompanied by a little explanation: looking down the Ks, for example, you find Kumlien is a narrow roman text from 1943 by Akke Kumlien, while

Krimhilde from 1934 was revealed to be by Albert Augspurg, a specialist in Schwabacher-style capitals.

For the most recent edition, marking its 55th anniversary, only W Pincus Jaspert was around to add new faces to the

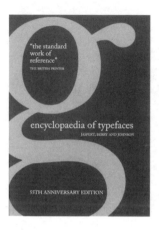

collection, and in his notes seems to be getting a little flummoxed by the task of cataloguing 2,000 fonts. 'Ceska Unicals on Page 43 and Unicala on Page 229 are the same,' he apologizes; 'Della Robbia on Page 65 was modelled on Florentine not Roman capitals. Monastic on Page 158 is really Erasmus Initials.' One can only empathize. It can be hard enough distinguishing Empiriana (1920) from Bodoni (late eighteenth century). With 2,000 alphabets, the task must be Herculean.

Even the jacket of the anniversary edition throws up a difficult query. It displays a huge red g against a purple background. It is a beautiful character – a double bowl, a fluid stroke, a perfect balance and a juicy comma of an ear, big enough to use as a handle. But which g is it? There are no clues on the jacket flaps, and 2,000 possible clues inside.

Identifying a particular font can be the most infuriating task, and designers can spoil their whole day by walking past a shop window and seeing something they can't name. It is far worse than trying to identify a song from a snippet of lyric or melody.

The lower-case g can be doubly perplexing, because it is usually the letter that gives the face away. For it is with the g that designers let themselves go. It is not usually where they will begin – that's often the a, n, h and p – but it is where a lot of big decisions are made with regards to history and expression. Will there be a simple loop (Futura), or a double bowl (Franklin Gothic)? Will the two bowls be cursive and varied in thickness (Goudy Old Style), or will they be uniform in width (Gill Sans)? Will the ear be level (Jenson) or droopy and tear-shaped (Century Schoolbook)? Will it taper (Bembo), or will it be flat (Garamond)? Will the upper bowl be more voluminous than the bottom one (Century Old Style) or vice-versa (Walbaum)? And what about the link between the bowls?

Spot the difference: the lower-case g in (top row from left) Futura, Franklin Gothic, Goudy Old Style, Gill Sans, Jenson; (bottom row from left) Century Schoolbook, Bembo, Garamond, Century Old Style, Walbaum

These are not arbitrary decisions, but are tied to the pedigree of the type. A transitional Baskerville style, for example ITC Cheltenham, will look odd if the quirky lower bowl of its g, which has a tiny gap at the top left, suddenly closes up. With script or larger display type, the discipline is still there, but now the imagination of the designer may take flight – the solid underlining slap of a Broadway g, the generous lower slurp of a Snell Roundhand g, the supersized lower bowl of a Nicholas Cochin g.

And so which g adorns the jacket of the encyclopaedia of all these gs? One can narrow it down by consulting another trustworthy tome, *Rookledge's Classic International Type Finder*. This breaks down hundreds of fonts according to the stresses, slopes, angles and serifs of individual letters, aiding both type identification and selection. So the g in question could be examined for its bowl, balance and ear, which eliminates about 670 specimens and leaves about thirty – including Aurora, Century Schoolbook, Bodoni Book, Corona, Columbia, Iridium, Bell, Madison and Walbaum. Walbaum looked to be the favourite for a while, but after much flicking back and forth through the pages, and looking extremely closely again, I wasn't so sure. It could also have been Iridium or Bodoni 135 or Monotype Fournier.

I turned to a more modern search option. Inevitably, the iPhone has an app for font identification, named *WhatTheFont*. It allows you to take a photograph of a letter or word; then to highlight that part of the photo (the g) you wish the app to identify. It then uploads this somewhere, and offers you a choice of possible font matches. For my encyclopaedia g it offered a great many, some of which were attractive modern types – Gloriola Display Standard Fat, Zebron, Absara Sans Head OT-Black, Deliscript Italic, and Down Under Heavy – but none of which came close to being correct. Trying this again, offering another g, a computer-rendered, 72-pt Georgia g, WhatTheFont actually FaredMuchWorse, suggesting it was almost every other font in the world apart from Georgia. It could be Phantasmagoria Headless, it conjectured, or Imperial Long Spike, or Two Fisted Alt BB.

Let down by the app, I tried the more traditional route of modern knowledge – the web – where you can consult a dedicated type forum at MyFonts.com (part of the Bitstream digital foundry site). The contributors here, who go under such names as listlessBean and Eychawk, display vast knowledge, an eagerness to help, and inestimable amounts of bile. Many sound as if Comic Book Guy from *The Simpsons* has been knocked over the head by heavy bound volumes of *Typographica*. Each day, as many as a hundred unidentified fonts are posted for identification and anyone can suggest a solution. The case is then marked solved or unsolved, or in some cases 'Not A Font' (because it's a logo or hand-drawn). On the day I spent too many hours browsing, people wanted to know the name of the fonts used for, to offer a small sample, Batman Gothic Knight, Bonnie Tsang

Photography, Perry Mason television titles and the Little Boulder Sweet Shop.

There was also a poser from 'digitallydrafted', who wanted to identify the Quiznos eatery tagline 'SUBS SOUPS SALADS'. This elicited eleven contributions, among them:

I'm starting to believe it is Verveine (alias Trash Hand) by Luce Avérous, with some letters customized (Gincis)

I got EXTREMELY close by modifying Tempus Sans ITC, rotating the S 180 degrees ... had to manually tweak the P and B (digitallydrafted)

Tempus Sans???????? You better take a closer look at TrashHand, that's all I can say for now ... (Gincis)

Looks like Good Dog (Jessica39180)

Sorry, Jessica, but it doesn't look like any of all the Good Dog fonts (neither Bad Dog or Family Dog). Did you take a look at them before posting? (Gincis)

And so it continued, until the crushing verdict was delivered: Not A Font.

Another engaging conundrum had been presented to the forum by Starbucks. One of the members was puzzled by the round green emblem with 'STARBUCKS COFFEE' in a bold and blocky typeface around the rim, white on green. It is one of the most identifiable logos in the world, but is it a custom font or something you can buy? It turned out that Starbucks was not a new query on the WhatTheFont forum. There were thirty-four others – ranging from the typeface on the Sumatra coffee bag to the face on the Christmas ads to an in-house promotion of the Cinnamon Dolce Latte. The logo font query had been submitted by macmaniacttt, and the first positive sighting was by terranrich, who tentatively suggested SG Today Sans Serif SH Ultra. But he wasn't really sure:

> All the characters match, but somehow it doesn't look exact. Maybe it's just my own eyes?

> Heron 2001 suggested that it WAS his eyes. 'The C is way off ... among other things ...'

> Terranrich then got all excited: 'I've found it!!! HAHA!! Finally! I got the vector logo from BrandsOfTheWorld. com, straightened out the letters manually, and then ran it through WhatTheFont. It's Freight Sans Black. :-D Case marked solved.'

Unfortunately, **Freight Sans Black** was designed by Joshua Darden in 2005, many years after Starbucks began. So Guess77 had some bad news: 'Case marked unsolved.' There was then a link to another hotbed of font analysis, *Typophile*. Here, one Stephen Coles laid everyone flat:

> The Starbucks logo was created many years before Freight was even a twinkle in Joshua Darden's eye.

Freight Sans Black is quite similar, but the Starbucks
ID is custom lettering, not a font. Note the differences
in the B and S.

It was true: the B had smaller fill-ins, and the S was curlier,
with a swell in the middle. Ah well. As Comic Book Guy
might say, 'I've spent my entire life trying to decipher a
typeface … and now there's only time left to say … Life well
spent!'

It was time to post my own Encyclopaedia 'g' query, and
I sat back and looked forward to spirited debate. There was
none, for within minutes Eyehawk had an answer.

Font identified as ACaslon Pro-Regular. Case marked
solved.

13

Can a Font be German, or Jewish?

There are, these days, even more encyclopaedic type directories than the *Encyclopaedia of Type Faces* – and the most encyclopaedic of them all is *FontBook*, a bright yellow doorstop published by FontShop, an agency founded in 1988 to sell digital types on floppy disks and more recently online. The book is quite a cult. Search for it on Google images and you will find a whole series of mash-up movie posters, with *FontBook* featuring in everything from *Braveheart* to *Lord of the Rings* ('ONE BOOK TO RULE THEM ALL, ONE BOOK TO FIND THEM').

A copy of the directory is sitting on a shelf in the Berlin office of Erik Spiekermann, FontShop's co-founder and a legend in the graphic design world. He is famously quoted as saying that while some men like to look at women's bottoms, he prefers type. The FontShop directory contains much to keep him happy – more than 100,000 fonts, ready for every conceivable (and inconceivable) use. They come from eighty-one type foundries and to make the choice for the harried advertiser or art director a little easier they have split them up into loose categories, rather like a wine list. There is the 'no-nonsense functionality' of sans serifs such as **Meta**, **DIN** and **Profile**, or the 'contemporary sensitivity of neo-traditional romans' such as Scala and Quadraat, and the 'streetwise novelty' of **Hands** and **Blur**. Or the 'Ironics': fonts like **STONED** (stoned – which conjures up an endless Grateful Dead gig) or *Falafel* (like a sign slapped onto the side of a Middle Eastern market cart) or `Trixie` (a typewriter whose ribbon should have been changed ten working days ago).

In the Display section of the catalogue, there are further oddities such as Kiddo Caps (an alphabet consisting of children doing things like brushing up beneath a budgie cage and flying a flag); NOOD.less (a bowl of noodle soup without the soup); BANANA.strip Regular (letters constructed from drawings of banana skins); Old Dreadful No 7 (an embarrassing collection of metal springs, fish, snakes, darts and backs of cats in the shape of an alphabet); or F2F Prototipa Multipla (unreadable and uninterpretable). Sometimes the names alone are enough to make you not want to go there: Elliott's Blue Eyeshadow; Monster Droppings; Bollocks; OldStyle Chewed; Hounslow.

There are also, of course, all the classic fonts, and among these are several faces that Spiekermann has created

The big yellow bible of the type world

himself — **FF Meta**, ITC Officina Sans and ITC Officina Serif and FF Info (ITC stands for International Typeface Corporation, FF stands for FontFont). These are the epitome of clean and efficient information — type that has helped define the look of Spickermann's home city of Berlin. An art historian by training, Spiekermann is the kind of designer whose enthusiasm for type and graphic systems permeates not just his own life, but almost everyone he comes into contact with. He is the type world's most prominent educator and proselytizer. He may have been the first to use a new word to describe his condition. 'Most people take the way words look for granted,' he said in a BBC film about cultural artefacts. 'Words are there to be read — end of story. Once however *typomania* sets in, it becomes quite a different story.'

Spiekermann's rise to prominence coincides precisely with the rise of digital type, and also with the reunification of Germany. His fonts adorn the Berlin Transit network and the Deutsche Bahn national railway, while a short walk from his office is the Philharmonie, the home of the Berlin Philharmonic, for whom Spiekermann designed the corporate branding. But that was a few years ago, and he isn't entirely happy with what's happened to it since. 'They fucked it up as quickly as they could,' he says. He describes his design for a grid system to be used by the in-house promotions and marketing people, a template in which he hoped 'the type could be freely organized, but still find its rhythm. Type has rhythm, just like music. But it's like cooking – you can follow a recipe to the last gram, but if the love isn't there it's just flat and bland.'

He's not very keen on the new posters either, preferring the images he gave them of landscapes. 'They said, "What does landscape have to do with music?" Like type, landscape and music are all about emotion. But that's the one thing about this job – I love to be a graphic designer, but could we get rid of clients somehow please?'

Spiekermann, who is in his early sixties, has also used type to define corporate identities for Audi, Sky TV, Bosch and Nokia. He hopes that his types will trigger associations with a product even before the company's name or logo is revealed, although he hopes that his involvement with a redesign of *The Economist* will have the opposite effect, keen to design type that is in effect invisible. 'I never want anyone to pick it up and say, "What a cool typeface." I want them to say, "What a cool article." I don't design the notes – that's what writers do; I do the sound. And the sound has to be legible.' For the German railways, Spiekermann and

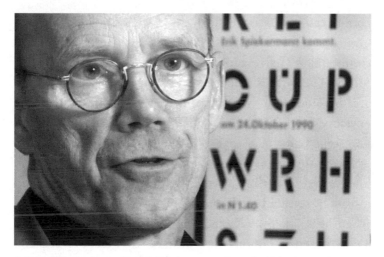

Self-confessed typomaniac Erik Spiekermann – from the *Helvetica* movie

his team had to make a family of typefaces to accommodate both fat headline type for advertising, and the much smaller text on the menus in the dining car. And even then there were variations. 'Wine menus look different from snack menus,' he says, 'because wine is more valuable – so that's serif. The snack menus are in sans serif.'

Spiekermann is one of those people for whom not being able to identify a g would be grounds for serious self-reappraisal. 'But I'm not quite as nerdish as I was. Perhaps it's age. In my generation I was the nerdiest of the nerds. But now with young kids – there are so many more nerds.' He says he became 'infected' himself at the age of six. He was living very close to a printshop in Lower Saxony and 'I saw all that messy metal type, and all that oily dirty ink, and then someone placed a pristine piece of paper on top of it and it produced this clean and clear text that you could read – it was magical, and I was hooked.' He was given the guillotined paper strips, which he used to draw trains and the narrow lorries his father drove for the British forces. Then in his teenage years, 'I had a crush on a girl, and I would write her letters and print her address on the envelopes. Other kids play with Lego, but I had some Futura and some Gill.'

His professional career began when he turned seventeen and moved to Berlin to avoid the draft. He began work as a printer, setting type by hand. He drew his first typefaces when he worked as a typographer in London in the late 1970s, based on famous fonts he used to collect in wood and metal. He wrote to his heroes for advice, including Matthew Carter, Adrian Frutiger and Günter Gerhard Lange. 'With Matthew and Adrian it was almost like the freemasons – it was them and a dozen others, and they were glad there were whippersnappers like me about because most people weren't interested. These days it's almost the other way round. Everybody wants to design a bloody typeface.'

Spiekermann teaches a course at the University in Berlin and says that he tells his students, above all other things, that digital type can be too harsh. 'When letters were cut from metal and wood there was a warmth, some fuzziness, that came about when it was printed. Now we have to *add* warmth to our letters, but we can't do it through the printing. So I add it by not making my type too perfect – I leave stuff alone, I won't make it mathematically, so it can look unfinished and handmade. Nylon can be perfect, but I'd rather wear wool, because it feels different on the skin on different parts of the body.'

Twenty years from now you will be more disappointed by the things that you didn't do than by the ones you did do. So throw off the bowlines. Sail away from the safe harbor. Catch the trade winds in your sails. Explore. Dream. Discover. – Mark Twain

Spiekermann's Meta font

He refers to his Meta font as an example. 'If you look at the data, it's a mess. The thickness is all over the place, nothing is identical. But I've resisted any attempt to clean it up, because then it wouldn't be Meta any more, it would be a mechanical clone. And that's the challenge for all of us – to create warmth in a digital world. Not many people can do it. You see a lot of stuff that looks great but simply doesn't turn you on. It's like making a song on a synthesizer. To make a drum machine sound good is really difficult – you might as well play real drums. We're still analogue beings. Our brains and eyes are analogue.'

Spiekermann's blog, which is called Spiekerblog, contains acerbic comments on type he sees on his travels. As well as Berlin, Spiekermann has offices in London and San Francisco, and as he flies around he observes how type defines not only a city, but the characteristics of a nation. He sees parallels with architecture – Bauhaus influencing the geometric **Futura** – the classic German sans serif font –

while tall British Victorian terraces reflect the serif tradition. And there are parallels in commerce. 'What does England make these days?' he asks. 'Jam, marmalade, cider, little pressies, gift stuff. English serifs have defined the packaging of tea. The French have defined perfume, the Italians have defined fashion, and we Germans have defined cars. Also everything in France is auto-shaped. Their typefaces look like a Citroën 2CV.'

In Germany, Erik Spiekermann, like all of his generation, was brought up reading and writing two scripts: the **old German gothic script** as well as regular roman type, and the duality defined the darkly confused relationship his country has had with type since type began.

The blackletter type first used by Gutenberg took on several forms with slight variations – **Textualis** or **Textura**, **Bastarda**, **Cursiva**, **Schwabacher** and **Fraktur** – though most of them died out as a popular form of text when the roman letter gradually assumed prominence throughout the sixteenth century. The heaviest, blackest blackletter type held fast to the work of courtly scribes: the elaborate swirling capital waves of ink with their internal crossbars, better suited to iron gates than paper, and the unforgiving jagged lower-case, devoid both of curves and signs of humanity, the reading of which is akin to sticking needles in one's eyes.

Their use today is largely confined to the confirmation of noble tradition, not least on Pilsner beers (Mexican beers as much as German faithfuls) and newspaper mastheads (The New York Times, Telegraph and Mail groups – and hundreds more throughout Europe and the US), or as a

The New York Times
Los Angeles Times
Irish Examiner
The Sydney Morning Herald
The Daily Telegraph

Blackletter news from around the world

Make mine a pint of blackletter – this Stiegl one is a modern revival

Blackletter metal: motörhead

measure of pastiche denoting posposity, grandeur and the presence of tourists (Ye Olde Pub sign, anything in Stratford-upon-Avon). The third use is a world unto itself: heavy metal (try writing motörhead or Christian Death Metal in jaunty Lucida Bright and see how many T-shirts you sell). And then there are tattoos: nothing says Menace quite like a word written in Old English.

But the German experience is different, and highly political. The use of Fraktur (a slightly less flamboyant gothic lettering than Schwabacher) continued in Germany well into the twentieth century, and in 1928 more than half of all books were still printed in blackletter. Its use had been advocated most vehemently at times of economic uncertainty, or when Germany struggled to define itself on the international stage. Deutsche Schrift, which had its strongest cultural roots in Martin Luther's Bible of 1523, became a talisman as strong as any flag or figurehead. Dissenting voices were largely drowned out, including the Brothers Grimm, who fearing for their literary reputation called Fraktur 'barbaric'.

But at the beginning of the twentieth century the move against gothic type gathered momentum, spurred on both by the demands of international trade and by the creative and political concerns of artists who had been influenced by Johnston and Gill in England and the broader sweep of the Italian Futurists and Bolsheviks. The type designer Paul Renner, whose dynamic sans serif Futura of 1927 defined the modernist movement, was at the centre of it. He renounced gothic text most vocally when the Nazi party embraced it (the Nazis judged roman text degenerate, believing only traditional gothic text could fully express the purity of the nation; a view not shared by the Italian fascists). Renner was arrested in 1933, having protested against the imprisonment of his teaching colleague Jan Tschichold, and directly after a lecture Renner gave about the history of letterforms, which the Nazis judged too sympathetic towards roman types. His arrest could hardly have been a surprise: when a magazine asked for his thoughts on graphic design, he observed that 'Political idiocy, growing more violent and malicious every day, may eventually sweep the whole of western culture to the ground with its muddy sleeve.'

Third Reich propaganda not only employed gothic lettering for its message, but made it the message itself: one slogan read 'Feel German, think German, speak German, be German, even in your script.' Perhaps overwhelmed by this onslaught, Renner made several attempts to combine gothic and roman type, while the Nazis evolved their own more brutish, angular and heroic Fraktur before the war; nicknamed 'the jackboot gothic', it was something that went typographically well with the swastika.

But in January 1941, everything suddenly changed. Gothic script was outlawed by decree, newly labelled 'Schwabacher-Jewish'. Centuries of tradition were cast aside overnight, the type being newly associated with the documents of Jewish bankers and the Jewish owners of printing presses.

Deutſche Schrift
iſt für die Auslandsdeutſchen eine unentbehrliche Schutzwehr gegen die drohende Entdeutſchung

Third Reich slogan. It reads: 'German Script. It is an indispensable protective weapon for Germans abroad against menacing de-Germanization.'

But the true reason was pragmatism. 'In the occupied territories you just couldn't read it,' says Erik Spiekermann. 'If you were French and saw a sign saying **Verboten** in Gothic, it could be very confusing. But the main reason was that the Germans just couldn't make enough of the stuff – there was a shortage of type.' When it came to printing outside Germany, the Nazis found few gothic fonts in French or Dutch foundries. And there was a further advantage: the roman-heroic architecture of Albert Speer could now employ Trajan-style inscriptions above their columns.

The switch to roman type outlived the ideology. After the war, Paul Renner declared that 'the motives that led to this step may have been loathsome, but this decree itself was an undeserved gift from the heavens, of the kind which occasionally deliver goodness from those whose intentions are bad.'

His own early type designs would become increasingly influential, although what he described as his 'inner emigration' in Germany after the war resulted in little new work. Interestingly, it was from Switzerland that the new international typefaces – Helvetica and Univers – emerged in the 1950s. The concentration of power had shifted: the present belonged to clean lines devoid of political or historical connotations, to an alphabet that looked the same throughout the new Europe, to a simple g that would be instantly recognizable without recourse to a typeface encyclopaedia.

This loss of a national type identity is obviously to be welcomed, in so far as it relates to the Third Reich. But the homogenization is regretted by many designers. As Matthew Carter recalled: 'Once I could be parachuted blindfold anywhere in the world, take the blindfold off and look around, and I could see the shop facias and newspapers, and I would know where I was just from the typeface. I'd see the type of Roger Excoffon [creator of Banco, Mistral and Antique Olive] and know that I had landed in France. But now a typeface is released in Tokyo or Berlin or London and it's gone around the world overnight, and it has completely lost its sense of origin.'

Futura

Futura – Paul Renner's most enduring work – is the best known of all German fonts. Commissioned in 1924, it belongs to an era before the Nazis, and still looks modern, more than eighty years on. It is a font that type fans feel passionate about: witness the controversy when IKEA dumped it in favour of Verdana.

Renner, a painter as well as a typographer and lecturer, developed Futura initially for a publisher, Jakob Hegner, who told him that he wanted something artistically liberating. The day after his visit, Renner began his first drafts, and the words with which he chose to experiment with his new type did not arrive by chance: **'die Schrift unserer Zeit'**, he wrote – the typeface of our time. He could just as easily have written **'Zeitgeist'**.

Renner worked in a golden age of fonts and in Futura he created a timeless type, forever suspended between irrefutable traditions and a vision of things to come. After its launch, Renner kept working to perfect it for four more years. But its influence was immediate. Renner reported that as early as 1925, much of the civic appearance of Frankfurt am Main was already set in Futura by order of the city's planning office. He also noted many similar typefaces appearing at that time, a fact he attributed to 'unthinkingly' showing his early work-in-progress to other

FUTURA
die Schrift unserer Zeit
BEGLEITE
das Bild unserer Zeit

Advertising material for Futura, showing Paul Renner working on his design

designers in a slide show, telling 'the whole world what had led me to this new type form'.

The font has proved resilient. Volkswagen, with its socialist marketing ideals, still uses Futura in its advertising, to a point where it would be dangerous to switch it, like tampering with the brakes. But the most famous appearance of Renner's visionary font, and his geometric interpretation of letters and numbers, is, suitably enough, in space. The Apollo 11 astronauts didn't just gather rocks and stick in a flag, they also left behind a plaque inscribed in Futura capitals. Did the short-sleeved people in Houston make Futura their positive choice for typographic reasons, or because the name suited the mission? Who knows. Ultimately it just looked right.

The signatures may be hard for extraterrestrials to read but they'll have no problem with the Futura

14

American Scottish

In some ways, the United States has never really thrown off the cloak of English type. The Declaration of Independence was printed in Caslon, and the *New Yorker* magazine still is. The *New York Times* still uses Times Roman and **Bookman**, and an Old English blackletter for its masthead. But the American type foundries of the nineteenth century gave things a very good shake.

The most influential of these established themselves in Philadelphia in the 1790s and denied all English associations. They were, after all, Scottish. Chief among them was the firm of Binny & Ronaldson, who started their business after acquiring the press that Benjamin Franklin had bought, twenty years earlier, for his grandson, from the French firm of Fournier. Archibald Binny had learned letter-cutting in Edinburgh but his partner James Ronaldson had been a biscuit baker – until he lost everything in a fire. Ronaldson handled the business end of their new operation, while Binny did more than any craftsman of his time to establish an early American identity in print. Not the least significant of their innovations was to produce a $ sign; previously, printers had used a long 'S'.

Binny & Ronaldson's best known font is Monticello, which they called Pica No 1. This was a modern hybrid of Baskerville and Caslon, a transitional face combining thin and thick strokes that proved instantly popular. It wasn't radical, but it was celebrated as an American product, and received a significant accolade when in 1810 it was used in Isaiah Thomas's *The History of Printing in America*.

Towards the end of the nineteenth century, Binny & Ronaldson became a cornerstone of the American Type Founders Company (ATF), an amalgam of twenty-three American type foundries. Their font re-emerged, too, and for a while seemed oddly English, being renamed Oxford. However, it was renamed Monticello, after Thomas Jefferson's residence, in the 1940s, when it was used to print his papers, and has gained recent popularity after a digital revival by Matthew Carter. The original matrices are now in the Smithsonian.

Many American book publishers, including Scribner and later Simon & Schuster, favoured what was known as Scotch Roman for their books, a slightly more modern transitional face showing heavy influences of Bodoni and Didot. When

Dear Sir   Monticello July 10. 22.
  Your favor of the 3ᵈ. is duly received and with it a
copy of the Specimen of your types, for which accept my thanks.
altho' increasing debility warns me that it cannot be long
before the transactions of the world will close upon me,
yet I feel ardent wishes for the continued progress of science
and the arts, and the consequent advancement of the happiness
of man. when I look back to Bell's edition of Blackstone (about
1773) and compare his with your types, and can by the progress
of the last half century estimate that of the centuries to come
I am cheared with the prospects of improvement in the human
condition, which altho not infinite are certainly indefinite.
a stiffened wrist, the consequence of a former dislocation, renders
writing slow and painful I can only add my prayers for the
general advancement of my country to the assurances of my
my great and friendly respects to yourself.

                                        Th Jefferson

    Mr. Ronaldson.

Thomas Jefferson's letter to James Ronaldson, expressing admiration for
his fonts – part of the 'continued progress of science and the arts, and the
consequent advancement of the happiness of man'.

the de Vinne Press published a specimen book in 1907 they
used Scotch Roman to explain why it was popular:

'Books are not made for show. Books are written
to be read and read easily, without discomfort or
annoyance. The conditions of printing that favour
easy reading are plain types, clear print and freedom
from surprises.'

At the start of the twentieth century another font did truly
define a new American look, but with a distinctly English

name: Cheltenham (known by most printers as Chelt). Designed in 1896 by Bertram Grosvenor Goodhue and Ingalls Kimball for a New York publisher, the Cheltenham Press, the typeface dominated American advertising and display for the next fifty years. A rugged and uncompromisingly heavy serif, it had relatively little stroke variation: its capital A with a misaligned apex, its G with an ungainly stub at its bottom right, its g notable for its broken lower bowl and its Q an unbroken one. It was promoted by both of the new mechanical casting processes Monotype and Linotype, which guaranteed widespread use, much as a tune will eventually appeal if played often enough. In 1906 it was sold to the printing trade as one might sell cigarettes or dubious linaments:

> A happy face is a face that gives joy, and the Cheltenham
> – so *apt*, so *fitting* – is this kind.

Cheltenham had been 'the type sensation of the year', the ATF advertisement claimed. 'Until now it is hardly possible to pick up a publication of any merit without a showing of the complete series of both the Cheltenham Old Style and the Cheltenham Italic ...'

Cheltenham – in a modern Linotype version. In 2003 Matthew Carter revived it for the *New York Times*

Like the catchy tune, its appeal waned. It was a fairly charmless face, reliable and pliable, but not beautiful, and the refined tastes of Madison Avenue in the 1950s probably got bored with it before the public did. However, in the 2003 redesign of the *New York Times*, it made its comeback, digitized by Matthew Carter, and employed in bold condensed forms for the paper's headlines.

Cheltenham's principal replacements in the 1950s were far uglier – a selection of lavish script fonts that looked as if they were handwritten, either by a drunken man from the advertising agency, or by some extravagant Elizabethan. Fortunately, the Swiss were at hand, and at the end of the 1950s America began its great love affair with Helvetica.

The most enduring modern American font – and the most likely to appear on our computer drop-down menus – is Franklin Gothic, a typeface named after Benjamin Franklin and first published in 1905. This was a sans serif face before the style became the rage in England through Johnston and Gill. The American definition of gothic is not the same as the European one: it may be a heavy type, but it has no connection with scribes or the German blackletter. Nor with heavy metal bands.

It was made by Morris Fuller Benton, a young star at ATF who created a family of fonts that remain ever present in newspapers and magazines. His Franklin Gothic font had its roots in the German Akzidenz Grotesk, and has survived all manner of fashionable and faddish political pressures. It is not geometric or mathematical or futuristic: it is wide and squat and sure of itself, a slightly less refined form of

Univers. It was the closest American type would get to Swiss type, and it was the type that finally threw off the straitjacket of Englishness. Things 'All-American' have a habit of using Franklin Gothic to press their case, be it the titles on the Rocky films or the block capitals on Lady Gaga's album **THE FAME MONSTER**.

Benton also cut some letters for Frederic Goudy, the American type designer who had the greatest impact on the textual tone of America in the first half of the twentieth century. Partly this was down to productivity: he designed more than 100 fonts, several of them site-specific, such as Saks (for the clothing store) and Californian (for the University of California Press). And partly this was down to a bit of self-promotion. Goudy had a reputation for fast living (cars and girls), and he was one of those rare things – a prolific type designer with a penchant for the jazz life.

This was rarely reflected in his work, which tended towards the buttoned-down. Goudy was more of a magpie than a modernizer, although he endeavoured to put his own twist on traditional inspirations. His most famous type was Goudy Old Style – a finely drawn but rather vulnerable font, nodding to the Renaissance with fluid base lines, nervy flourishes and the most delicate serifs; it is still in wide usage, including *Harper's* magazine.

Goudy's most unusual font was 𝕲𝖔𝖚𝖉𝖞 𝕿𝖊𝖝𝖙 (1928), a blackletter with its heart in Gutenberg's Bible that stands quite apart from American trends. Goudy became obsessed with producing challenging variations of blackletter, and he was finicky about the results. Delivering a notorious invective regarding the type, he stated that anyone who would

Goudy Text and Goudy Italic characters –
playfully co-opted by William Barrett for his
series of images called 'My Type of People'

letterspace blackletter would 'shag sheep' – a phrase that
has also been applied, in the design world, to letterspacing
in lower case. (The German designer and head of Fontshop,
Erik Spiekermann, co-wrote a book called *Stop Stealing
Sheep & Find Out How Type Works*). Why is inappropriate
letterspacing so despicable? Because it looks ugly, and
because anyone skilled in typography takes immeasurable
offence at anything that insults their vision of beauty. Quite
right too.

Goudy left us other keen thoughts, too, including a
description of type design that encapsulates many of the
dilemmas, inspirations and heartbreaks of his trade. 'It is
hardly possible to create a good typeface that will differ
radically from the established forms of the past,' he wrote

Frederic Goudy at work

in his book *Typologia* in 1940. 'The perfect model for a type letter is altogether imaginary; there is no copy for the designer today except the form created by some earlier artist, and the excellence of a designer's work depends entirely upon the degree of imagination and feeling he can include in his rendition of that traditional form.'

Intriguingly, similar concerns were expressed by the Italian type designer Giambattista Bodoni almost two hundred years before. 'Letters do not achieve their true beauty when done in haste and discomfort,' the creator of the classic Bodoni font wrote, 'nor when done with diligence and pain, but only when they are created with love and passion.'

Moderns, Egyptians and Fat Faces

Was the TIGER WOODS scandal a little too grubby for the glossy magazines? Not if his first name was set in a huge capitalized version of BODONI on the cover of *Vanity Fair*. Then the story would look sophisticated, classy and refined.

Giambattista Bodoni of Parma and the Parisian Firmin Didot are the designers credited with inventing the 'Modern' class of typefaces in the eighteenth century, building on the 'Transitional' Baskerville, by introducing even greater contrast between thin and thick lines and long, fine serifs. These faces appeared in the 1790s, when improved printing techniques and paper quality enabled the punchcutter to cut far thinner strokes without a risk of cracking or disappearing on the page. If they then attached a ball to the J or the k, or sharpened the apex of A, they were confident that it wouldn't be chipped off. Didot and Bodoni both developed fonts that became increasingly extreme in their stroke contrasts (the U and V looking particularly vulnerable), while also flattening serifs and increasing the height of their narrow capitals.

The Moderns were designed primarily as book faces, and can look impressive with generous leading. But when increased to

Bodoni – always fit for purpose

display size there may be no finer example of the letterfounders' art. Certainly there is no quicker way of saying CLASS, which is why you still find them so prominent in *Elle*, *Vogue* and all the high-end fashion magazines.

Among the other great modern faces, the German nineteenth century Walbaum is still a romantic stunner today. Named after its creator Justus Erich Walbaum, it has the usual high-hat letters but also a softer and more approachable manner, and a very technical k that looks to have fallen from another font by mistake. Fairfield, Fenice and De Vinne also owe a lot to what have become known collectively as Didone faces, while the digital variants have introduced text sizes that have slightly reduced the letter contrast.

But where could type go after these extremes? Intriguingly it went the other way – to fonts that were fat, heavy and ungainly, to fonts that soaked up ink and boasted of their gluttony and pride. The industrial revolution was not only a thing of steam and speed, but also of grind and grime, and typefaces reflected mostly the latter. The scale of industrial and technological progress left no time for delicacy, and so the refined types of earlier centuries were discarded, replaced by letters as thickset as the participants in the bare-knuckle prizefights they would advertise. The fonts of this time – marketed with no-nonsense

The Victorian poster, packed with Fat Face and Egyptian fonts, that inspired John Lennon's 'For The Benefit of Mr Kite'.

English names like Thorowgood, Falstaff, Figgins Antique – screamed for your attention like the plumpest towncryer.

These fonts, which the trade grouped as Fat Face and Egyptian, had a ruggedness suited not only to the clank and heave of the new factories (they looked particularly good on the side of pump engines), but also to the din of the fairground and early Victorian music hall. The designs would inspire many forms of flowery ornamental woodtype, but we look at them now and see mainly men in top hats with dangling watch-chains; big fat type that refuses to be modernized.

GOTHAM IS GO

'I am not bound to win,' Barack Obama said on the eve of the vote of his historic healthcare reform bill in March 2010, 'but I am bound to be true.' It was a spoken address, but it came out of his mouth as if it had been **WRITTEN IN GOTHAM.**

There are some types that read as if everything written in them is honest, or at least fair. We have been conditioned to look at Times New Roman that way, and the same goes for Gotham, which was made in 2000 by Tobias Frere-Jones for Hoefler & Frere-Jones, one of the leading type design companies in New York City (or Gotham City, as Batman fans like to call it). The font bumbled along nicely for them for several years, gaining increasing popularity as a type that managed to look both establishment and fresh, and then, at the beginning of 2008, it got the sort of boost that no type designer would even dare dream of.

'We actually found out that the Obama campaign was using it by seeing it on TV,' Frere-Jones says, as if he still can't believe his luck. 'There was a rally in Iowa, and he was on a podium and all these people were waving signs, and the type on the signs was awfully familiar.' Obama wasn't alone: at that point in the primary there were still seven or eight candidates, and John Edwards was also using Gotham. But as Edwards and eventually Hillary Clinton dropped away, Frere-Jones was excited to see that the Obama campaign was not only still using his font, but that it had been installed at the heart of the candidate's graphic vision. 'In the past,' he explains, 'campaigns would have one logo, and then choose a number of typefaces to go with the advertisements and the banners and the website. But the Obama campaign put the same discipline into planning its look that would go into a big corporate identity. The campaign looked the same on election day as it did eighteen months before at the caucuses.'

As Obama's presidential bid gained momentum, Frere-Jones received nice emails from friends wondering whether he had seen his work employed in this important way. Gary Hustwit, the director of the *Helvetica* movie, sent him a picture of Obama, microphone in hand, standing in front of a banner that read, all in capitals, '**CHANGE WE CAN BELIEVE IN**'. In the next year, all the dynamic Obama watchwords – **CHANGE, HOPE, YES WE CAN** – would appear in these simple sans serif letters, notable for their solidity and durability. They also had unremarkability

A font to believe in? Yes We Can Trust Gotham

and inoffensability – a type consciously chosen to suggest forward thinking without frightening the horses. Gotham replaced the Obama team's original choice Gill Sans, which was discarded as too staid and inflexible (Gotham was available in more than forty varieties, Gill Sans in fifteen). 'Great choice,' observed Alice Rawsthorn in the *New York Times*. 'No typeface could seem better suited to a dynamic, yet conscientious, American public servant.' Rawsthorn also detected 'a potent, if unspoken, combination of contemporary sophistication (a nod to his suits) with nostalgia for America's past and a sense of duty'.

'That was certainly one of the qualities we set out to capture – that feeling of authority,' Frere-Jones says. (Frere-Jones also carries a sense of authority, a type archetype with glasses, neat apparel and a proper hair parting.) 'When we were developing it we realized it could be very contemporary, but also classic and almost severe.' In this respect at least it is comparable with Helvetica. 'We wanted to seize the chance to give it that range of voices, so it wasn't going to be a performer that could only really sing one song.'

But what if that performer had been batting for the other side? What if Gotham had been used in a campaign its maker disapproved of – would he have any way of objecting? 'Not once they had paid for it. That did happen. The Republican Senate candidate in Minnesota, Norm Coleman, had a website to raise money for his recount campaign, and that was in Gotham Medium and Gotham Bold all-caps, exactly the same as the Obama website. I felt personally annoyed, but the guy lost anyway, so ...'

Gotham was originally designed for *GQ* magazine, and was inspired by the letters over the entrance to the New York Port Authority Bus Terminal, one of the many three-dimensional vernacular signs threatened by the ravages of weather and time, and by the creeping uniformity of type made possible, easier and cheaper by digital technologies. Frere-Jones calls the pedigree and practicality of these letters 'non-negotiable', but because they were disappearing, he made it his weekend hobby to photograph as many as possible before it was too late. In four years he thinks he got every interesting letter and sign block from southernmost Battery Park to 14th Street, some 3,600 pictures. The joy was in finding lots of regional and international variations, including a particular style of geometric sans serif that only exists in Chinatown.

Gotham was originally designed for *GQ* magazine. So this is perfect unity: the font, the magazine, the President.

The only preservation Frere-Jones witnessed was when a new sign was bolted over an old one.

More than a year into Obama's presidency, Frere-Jones and his colleague Jonathan Hoefler can afford to be modest about Gotham's attributes, but during the campaign they were in pickier mood. 'Gotham isn't pretending to be anything it's not,' their website claimed in February 2008. 'The only thing Gotham works hard at is being Gotham.' But the same couldn't be said for Obama's competitors, both of whose choices carried bruised baggage. Hillary Clinton's principal campaign poster had her name in **New Baskerville bold**, the font that often confers a legal endorsement. John McCain used the 1950s sans serif Optima, perhaps an attempt to remind voters of his war record (Optima is the type on the Vietnam Veterans Memorial in Washington DC).

'Hillary's snooze of a serif might have come off a heart-healthy cereal box, or a mildly embarrassing over-the-counter ointment,' Jonathan Hoefler wrote in his blog. 'If you're feeling generous you might associate it with a Board of Ed circular, or an obscure academic journal. But Senator McCain's typeface was positively mystifying: after three decades signifying a very down-market notion of luxe, this particular sans serif has settled into being the font of choice for the hygiene aisle.'

How were these things done in earlier years? In 1948, the year the United Kingdom introduced its own revolutionary healthcare bill in the form of the National Health Service, the last thing one would have expected from the governing Labour Party would have been an interest in fonts. There were important housing and education reforms to consider, and new foods to ration, but at some point during this radical programme someone influential decided that none of it would make a good impression unless it was presented to the nation in a carefully considered and extremely boring typeface.

This man was Michael Middleton, a graphic designer and Labour loyalist, who believed that the right choice of font could be a vote winner. Three years after the war, he published a lavishly illustrated manifesto called *Soldiers of Lead*, a call for unity among typefaces and a blast against anything fancy or debauched. Type had to reflect the austerity of the day; all the better if it had a sturdy and traditional serif. Even the title of Middleton's pamphlet spoke of history. The full phrase reads: 'With twenty-five soldiers of lead I have conquered the world!' A centuries old paean to the power of movable type, it dates from the days before the letter J became the last addition to the alphabet.

Before Middleton's intervention, most Labour literature resembled a cramped and crowded meeting room in which everyone was remonstrating at once. In 1946, a poster suggesting one should 'Vote Labour for Progress' used six different fonts in as many sizes, as if it had been constructed from sweeping up the discarded type on a printer's floor. Despite the great promises of fonts like Johnston, Futura and Gill Sans, poster typography in Britain in the 1940s was still dominated by the blocky Fat Faces of the Victorians, and the Victorians, as we have seen, had shown no regard for typography at all.

What do these letters represent ? They have their
origins in medieval hand-drawn characters – have they
any place in the twentieth century ?

What happens to the ' recognition characteristics ' of
individual letters when they are elongated or squashed ?
Can you distinguish these at a slight distance ?

The top line of letters here are Victorian, the remainder
are more recent. Are they beautiful or are they ridiculous? Is it ' clever ' to depart from the essential basic
shape of a letter as much as these do ?

Michael Middleton's
admonishments on
unsuitable type, from
Soldiers of Lead

Middleton's manifesto proposed to keep everything light, simple and clear. 'Mistrust any type of "novel" design,' he advised his party faithful. Never use letters which are so condensed that 'they have the appearance of striped wallpaper'. The typefaces favoured were all safe bets: Bembo, Caslon, Times New Roman, Baskerville, Goudy, Perpetua and Bodoni. You could combine them in almost any combination and not go wrong so long as there was enough space between the lines.

Did *Soldiers of Lead* have any effect on Labour's fortunes? It is hard to judge. When petrol rationing was ended with some fanfare in 1950, the posters were set in plain Times Roman, whereas in previous years similar events were heralded in Chisel (a deep cut gravestone style) or Thorne Shaded (a grand *trompe-l'oeil* raised-letter font more suited to announcing the end of the Boer War). But Labour's narrow electoral majority of 1950 was wiped out the following year, the public voting in Churchill for a last hurrah.

The mid-century Conservative Party seemed to care little about type reform; if the serifs could have grown any flatter and steadier on Caslon or Baskerville they would have chosen them. But they had arrived at a universal font truth: we tend to treat the traditional and familiar as trustworthy. We are dubious of fonts that alert us to their difference, or fonts that seem to be trying too hard. We don't like being consciously sold things, or paying for fancy design we don't need.

Not much has changed over the years. The political manifestos of today are increasingly nervous documents, printed largely in Arial and Century; we read them with a cynical air, aware that we have read their type before. Michael Middleton died in the summer of 2009, aged ninety-one, having enjoyed a successful career away from the Labour Party running the Civic Trust and writing art reviews for the *Spectator*. He probably would have been amused by the cover of the Labour Party manifesto the following year, promising, in something very close to Arial – 'A future fair for all' – backed by a 1950s vision of a nuclear family admiring a bright sunrise (or sunset). But he would have approved, typographically at least, of the Conservative's 'INVITATION TO JOIN THE GOVERNMENT OF BRITAIN'. The cover of this document was text-only, and it looked very much like Baskerville. The Liberal Democrats, meantime, played it straight down the middle with a manifesto, posters, website and iPhone app in Helvetica.

Gotham inscription at the Freedom Tower

In the United States, Gotham has come to signify more than just change. You will find it on the inscription on the cornerstone laid for the new Freedom Tower at Ground Zero, and, despite its creator's claims that Gotham is just Gotham, it has inherited loaded associations with victory and honest success. Those who keep a keen eye on the fontography of movie posters have noticed that Trajan and Gill Sans have found a serious rival when it comes to movies that have a shot at the Academy Awards. There are many other noteworthy and more exciting fonts in the Hoefler & Frere-Jones catalogue (not least Vitesse, Tungsten and their classic version of Didot), but only one that features on the posters of **A Single Man**, **The Lovely Bones** and **Invictus** that decorate their office: we have chosen to spell out our new age of austerity in Gotham.

And finally there is the ultimate tribute, that point when you know your typeface has really joined the pantheon of the greats. This is the point where people decide not to pay for it. A package of eight Gotham weights costs $199 for use in one computer, with reductions for more machines, so people have tried to counterfeit the look as best they can. It will always be cheaper to use the free fonts on your computer, as Tobias Frere-Jones discovered when he searched for Obama memorabilia on eBay. There were posters promoting the usual messages of 'Hope – **Stand With Obama**' and 'Be The Change', and they had familiar layout and colours. But they looked slightly wrong in Gill Sans and Lucida, and they only fooled some of the people some of the time.

16 *Pirates* and Clones

In 1976, Max Miedinger, the original draughtsman of Helvetica, the world's most familiar font, revealed that, like most type designers at that time, he received a set fee for his work, and failed to reap royalties. 'Stempel earns a lot of money with it but I am out of the game,' he said. 'I feel cheated.' The Swiss typographer died virtually penniless, four years later.

Stempel, Helvetica's font foundry owner, has clearly made money from the font. But not perhaps as much as you might expect. Owning fonts is not as lucrative as, say, licensing Microsoft programs, for the simple reason that if your font is any good, it gets copied. And there is very little you can do about it. Helvetica clones have been available for decades, often with tiny modifications. Fonts such as Akzidenz Grotesk Book and **Nimbus Sans Bold** display similar attributes to Helvetica; one clone even calls itself Swiss. But the biggest transgressor, in terms of global impact, is Arial.

Arial is the Helvetica lookalike favoured by – you can probably guess this – Microsoft. In texts and documents, it has almost certainly seen more use than the original. Many people will prefer it to Helvetica, for it has a slightly softer and more rounded tone. Without actually mentioning Helvetica, Arial has always sold itself on these attributes, drawing attention to its fuller curves and angled terminals, and claiming it is less mechanical and industrial than other sans serifs. These 'humanist' characteristics ensured it was 'more in tune with the mood of the last decades of the twentieth century'.

A remarkable thing about Arial is that it has many deliberate differences that – when you get used to them – are as different from Helvetica as pineapple is from mango. The a on Helvetica has a more prominent tail and a horizontal rather than vertical bar. There is no vertical descender on Arial's G. The bar on Arial's Q is wavy not straight.

But Arial is still regarded – and rightly so – as a cheat. It was consciously designed in the early 1980s to offer an alternative to Helvetica before Microsoft bundled it with its Windows operating system – specifically as a printer font to rival those bundled with Adobe's exclusive software. Helvetica was owned by Linotype, so it was to be expected that Monotype would offer an alternative. But it wasn't just the comparable looks that irked the design community, it was the fact that its width and other key elements fitted exactly the same grids that Helvetica occupied, thus making it interchangeable in any amount of documents and printing or display software.

When Microsoft took advantage of this in Windows 3.1 it did so because Arial was cheaper than Helvetica, and it wanted to save money on the licence fee. A sound business decision, unless one objected to the principle of capitalizing on another's artistry. Monotype was not acting illegally, and in any case maintained – with some justice – that Arial was an updated version of their own Grotesque series from more than a century earlier.

Few of the millions who use Arial care. But among the design community, Arial retains bad blood. There is even a video on the Arial–Helvetica stand-off from CollegeHumor (google 'Font Fight'). This is quite an elaborate story set in a warehouse, and features Helvetica's gang – Helvetica herself (female, smart), alongside a motley male gathering

Helvetica

C G R a r t

Arial

C G R a r t

of Playbill (unshaven, Western), **STENCIL** (General Patton), Braggadoccio (Italian tenor), Jazz LET (cool black dude) and American Typewriter (wired reporter). Within moments they are confronted by Arial's gang – Arial is glamorous and boastful, Tahoma is a Red Indian, Vivaldi is sophisticated, Papyrus is Egyptian and gay, and PartyLET likes his beer.

'Arial!' Helvetica says. 'I haven't seen you since … since you cloned me and stole my identity!' There are other little scores to settle: 'Playbill, you took my land, you killed my family.' 'What are you gonna do about it, Tahoma – a raindance?' Soon they are fighting, and Helvetica punches Arial to the ground. There is a late arrival in a colourful superhero outfit: 'Comic Sans is here to save the day!' There's no response, as everyone is already dead. 'If anyone needs me,' he says sheepishly, 'Comic Sans will be over here …'

In another CollegeHumor video ('Font Conference'), the same actors appear as different characters (Baskerville Old Face, Old English) to debate the granting of membership to Zapf Dingbats.

Hermann Zapf, the real life creator of these symbols (which include legions of arrows, scissors, crosses and star shapes), does not, understandably, have much of a sense of humour regarding the pirating of his own work. In the 1970s, Zapf used the emergence of photocomposition to advance the cause of the lone unprotected artist and emphasize the threat of unlawful copying. He couldn't have foreseen the full impact of the computer age on his craft, but his call for greater protection was prescient. And it fell on deaf ears.

Just a small selection of the huge array of Zapf's dingbats

In October 1974, Zapf addressed the Library of Congress Copyright Office in Washington DC and made a heartfelt plea for greater protection. He observed that for about 450 years copying types had been an expensive and time-consuming business, as each would have to be cut by hand in the same manner as the original. Immense skill was needed to make a credible reproduction, and the possibility of fraud was therefore limited to a small handful of professionals.

In the nineteenth century, with the invention of the electrotyping machine in New York, theft became a little easier. Punchcutting was bypassed as moulds could be made directly, but this was still a highly skilled process and hugely expensive if one wanted to produce a range of weights (and we should remember that in any one weight, the basic alphabet was just the beginning; in every medium, bold or italic, there would be at least 150 characters or glyphs, including all the accents, ligatures, numbers and punctuation.) As late as 1963, the Parisian foundry owner Charles Peignot estimated that to make a full family of twenty-one weights would cost about 3.3m francs.

Hermann Zapf noted that court cases had rarely decided in favour of the designer. In 1905, the Federal Court in Washington heard a complaint from the American Type Founders Company that their Cheltenham range (which had cost them $100,000 to make) had been copied by the letterpress manufacturer Damon & Peets, but their claim failed. Shortly afterwards, Caslon Bold appeared in the courts, as the Keystone foundry of Philadelphia unsuccessfully tried to protect their type against a piratical publisher. And then the prolific Frederic W Goudy also got fed up with seeing his types employed in situations where they had no licence (and he received no royalties), and he also sued, also without success and at great personal cost. The courts' ruling in all these cases was: type is in the public domain, and has no characteristics other than utility. In Goudy's case, the court found that 'a design for a font of type is not patentable subject matter.'

And so it remains. There is a little more protection now in Europe, but in the US – the biggest single market – an alphabet cannot be protected. Or rather it can be protected only if each individual character – every italic condensed 'a', every ampersand and umlaut, every fraction and ornament – applies for and is granted its own patent. Given that many digital alphabets now have more than 600 such glyphs, this is almost impossibly time-consuming and devastatingly expensive, and only in a case such as Helvetica could it ever hope to pay dividends. For the other 100,000 or so less popular types, the most one can protect is the name,

Hermann Zapf, campaigner for type rights

and the computer programming code that enabled the type to be made.*

Zapf's pleas make as valid point today as they did when he presented them in the mid-1970s. 'To make a living as a freelance designer, believe me, you have to work hard with your mind and with your hand,' he told the City University in New York. 'You want to earn at least enough money to dress your beloved wife nicely, to feed your children every day, and to live in a house where the rain does not drop on your drawing pad.' He said that these necessities were becoming increasingly hard to come by, because the basic financial arrangements accepted in other art forms were not accepted in his. He used the example of Leonard Bernstein recording a new version of *West Side Story* for Columbia Records: Bernstein would get royalties, and if an unscrupulous smaller record company tried to pass it off as their own under the name of another orchestra and conductor they would be severely dealt with by copyright protection and the legal system. But type designers were more like apple growers cultivating unique fruit without protective fences; whenever someone

---

* One of the few examples of successful typeface protection came in 1998, when Adobe won its case against Southern Software Inc and others. Adobe argued that not only had its fonts been copied, but the Utopia software that created them had been copied too, leading to a new law prohibiting this.

stole them, they could argue that apples were the result of the sun and rain and God's own fair intervention.

The alphabet as a free-for-all is an appealing concept, not least for lawmakers who fear the restriction of free speech (and the complex possibilities of distinguishing one lower-case 'g' from another). Zapf argued his case at a time when he believed there were 7,000 to 8,000 different typefaces, and he claimed, 'I hold the world record for the most type designs copied without permission.' In 2010, with the number of faces rather greater, and Zapf into his nineties and no longer designing, the title may still be his. But he has serious competition. Matthew Carter's acknowledged revivals of classic types have themselves been 'revived' or cloned. He manages to take a magnanimous view, a view that perhaps only the very successful can afford to take.

'Yes, there have been some horrible fights and rivalries,' he says, 'but generally speaking we all get on pretty well. I've got a friend in the fashion business who probably earns six times what I do. But there are a lot of really shitty people in the fashion business because there's a lot of money in there. In type design there is not a lot of money, and that's not what drives you. There are quarrels sometimes because somebody thinks someone's ripped off their work, and very often they're right. There are unscrupulous people in our business, but by and large people are fairly even tempered.'

Carter makes a distinction between the Helvetica clone from a company like Monotype that should know better and the designer with their head full of inadvertent influences from 550 years of history. 'It's happened to me that I'll be working on something and suddenly I'll look at it and think, "Wait a minute, I'm running into trouble here." So I'll call a designer up and say, "With the best possible motives I find myself encroaching on something you've already done – is that a problem?" And generally the answer has been "No". Most of us have a pretty good idea if we're getting too close to something. And I've had designers coming to me, and most of the time I don't mind.'

Carter says he learned something valuable some years ago on a visit to Ronnie Scott's jazz club in London. He went to see the drummer Elvin Jones, who was once with John Coltrane. 'He was part of the sainthood,' Carter says, 'and that night, he walked out before his set and announced that Buddy Rich had died that day. Here's me, thinking I know about music, and I would have said, "Buddy Rich was a wunderkind, vaudeville, clownish, white, big band, and a show-off – how could Buddy Rich and Elvin Jones ever have anything in common?" But Jones came out and said some very moving things. It taught me a lesson. Two drummers have things in common.'

At FontShop in San Francisco, they tend to use two methods to determine whether a newly submitted typeface is different enough for them to promote and sell: their eyes, and font-editing software such as Fontographer. If they think something looks familiar they will open up two fonts in Fontographer and compare the new with its inspiration. They will enlarge each letter and examine its coordinates, and if the edges of the points in a few letters are identical, then they will investigate further. 'It really is difficult to do something completely new,' says FontShop's type director Stephen Coles. 'My view is that if a new face isn't adding something to the landscape, then it's not going to be something that we would want to sell. But there are battles all the time.'

A recent example concerned Segoe, created by Monotype and licensed to Microsoft, which bears a close relationship to Frutiger. Their common usage is different (Segoe for screen display at small sizes, Frutiger for signage), and they do not share the same digital width vectors like Helvetica and Arial, but their obvious similarity caused widespread disquiet in design circles. Some of the outrage was spurred by the

Segoe UI
The quick brown fox jumped over the lazy dog.

fact that the main culprits were Microsoft, every creative's favourite whipping-corp (if they are happy to ignore the fact that Microsoft commissioned some of the best screen fonts in common use, not least Georgia from Matthew Carter).

Stephen Coles and other type bureau people have more immediate worries: counterfeit or illegally copied fonts sold cheaply or available free at many dubious outlets. One can buy unlicensed fonts not only from online sites that look like honest concerns, but also from the same peer-to-peer download sites that offer shared music and films. Allan Haley, the Director of Words and Lettering at Monotype Imaging, has detected that most graphic designers do not set out to steal fonts, but may borrow fonts from colleagues without checking their origin or paying a licence fee. (Most genuine sites license their digital fonts to be used by a specified number of computers and printers – the greater the number, the more you pay; there will also be more expensive and elaborate corporate deals.) 'Unfortunately, there are probably more illegal or pirate font distribution websites than there are legitimate sites,' Haley has suggested in his blog at fonts.com. 'They are run by people with no regard for the intellectual property rights of others. Eradicating these pirate sites is like trying to control a virulent fungus ... Most of us wouldn't consider buying a television off the back of a semi-trailer. Buying from a font pirate would be doing essentially the same thing.'

But even worse than that would be to use a pirated font on a campaign promoting anti-piracy. That would be really thoughtless, wouldn't it?

In the second week of January 2010, the unfortunate people at HADOPI, the French government agency charged with the promotion of copyright protection on the Internet, woke up to a marketing disaster so huge and absurd that they may not have believed it was actually happening. The typeface they had chosen to promote their campaign on posters, film and all other communications, and which was called Bienvenue, turned out to be something they had no right to use. They couldn't have licensed it legally either, because the font was an exclusive custom font designed for France Telecom.

Bienvenue was designed in 2000 by Jean François Porchez, an energetic designer whose Porchez Typofonderie was responsible for the digital look of a fair part of France's media and corporate branding. As well as providing the current face of the Paris Métro (**Parisine**), the company sold such designs as Parisine Office, Le Monde Sans, Le Monde Livre, and Apolline, the names themselves enough to transport you to the Place de la Concorde with *café crème* in hand. As is the norm these days, each alphabet will contain at least 600 glyphs, and would take many months to perfect. The fonts cost from €210 for use on up to eight machines to €8,640 for use on up to 5,000 machines – ie everyone catered for from the smallest design studio to a multinational company.

Sadly, the anti-piracy agency HADOPI couldn't license Bienvenue no matter what the rates. Jean François Porchez had made the font in several weights exclusively for France Telecom in 2000, and since it was intended both for internal company use and branding, it was widely seen. It was also admired, particularly for the soft harmony of the letters and the warmth that the rounded strokes conveyed.

Plan Créatif, the design consultants charged with making the logo for HADOPI, obviously admired it too, as was made clear when it was unveiled by the French Ministry for Culture and Communication. The similarity was initially spotted by a designer who used to work for Typofonderie Porchez, and the word spread rapidly among the design community until it reached the mainstream media. Plan Créatif then started to backtrack, and disastrously so. It claimed that the use of the typeface was only intended as a draft, and had somehow been subject to 'erroneous digital manipulation'. Three days after the logo was first unveiled, the agency announced that it was in a position to present its other, proper version. This was indeed a little different, and used the typeface **FS Lola**, designed by the London company Fontsmith.

One was then left to decide whether Plan Créatif had made a genuine mistake, or had performed a volte-face after it had been exposed. One answer came by checking the records at the French National Institute for Intellectual Property, which showed that its logo had been registered for official (ie not draft) use six weeks earlier. And another came when the graphic design writer Yves Peters and other bloggers decided to take matters further by calling Fontsmith and asking precisely when Plan Créatif had purchased FS Lola. They said that it was 'rush-ordered' on the very day the new logo was exposed.

There was yet another revelation to come. The logo was accompanied by red text, which explained what the initials HADOPI stood for: *Haute Autorité pour la diffusion des oeuvres et la protection des droits sur Internet*. This appeared in the same font a week apart, beneath both the original and the new logo – **Bliss** by the London designer Jeremy Tankard. When was Bliss ordered? On the same day as FS Lola; its original use had also been unlicensed.

Jean François Porchez says he partially enjoyed the irony: 'It makes me smile.' But only partially. 'At the same time we need to find the best possible solution for this problem.' In other words, his lawyers were on the case.

Optima

Hermann Zapf will always be remembered for his dingbats. But the German designer is also responsible for some of the twentieth century's most exacting typefaces, among them Palatino, Melior, **SAPHIR** and *Zapfino* – the latter one of the most fluid and effective calligraphic fonts. But it is his Optima typeface that stands out.

Zapf was born in Nuremberg, and when he was young he wanted to become a chimney sweep; he particularly liked the prospect of getting his hands black for a career. He worked as a cartographer in the war, and then established his reputation as a designer at the Stempel foundry in Frankfurt. His first hit was Palatino in 1949, influenced by classic Italian types and displaying the quirks of a stonemason and formal penman. It had regular serifs and strokes of fairly even width, but it also had a loop on the capital P that wouldn't join up, and an e that had a bit chipped off on the right of its bowl. The font is consistently crisp and reassuringly humanizing; its digital version still works today as an appealing everyday text alternative to Georgia.

But when Zapf published Optima nine years later, it looked as if it had come from another planet. It took him more than three years to design, and it was three more before the first sizes

Optima – a perfect perfume font

appeared in the Stempel foundry specimen book. It is a highly original piece of work, a hybrid between something respectfully Roman in stature and something modern and sans serif in form. There were thirty years between Futura and Optima, but they shared a distinct sharp-edged German modernism. Optima was originally designed as a display font, but it is also highly legible as a text face; the only disadvantage of viewing it small is a loss of subtlety at the tip of each of its straight lines, which have both a slight swelling and a gentle indentation. But it is this swelling and this rivulet that renders the type beautiful. It is comparable to Albertus in its ability to withstand a prolonged period of admiration.

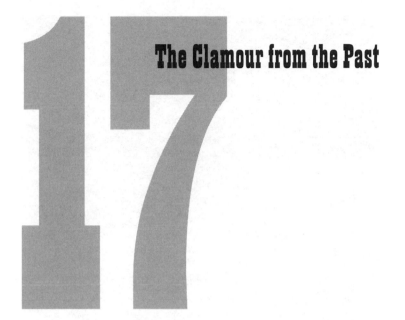

The Clamour from the Past

'**E**very single page is an absolute miracle,' declares Sue Shaw in her office at the Type Archive – a converted horse hospital in Lambeth, south London. She is sitting in front of glass cases holding the sort of moulds Gutenberg would have used to make his Bible, while on the table in front of her are bills and a chequebook and architects' plans.

In her hand is an eighteenth-century German law book. It is eight inches deep, the index is 314 pages and the type is tiny, crammed into thin columns with no breathing space. Each letter has been cast by hand and then placed in a typecase with thousands of other letters, page by page, 3,000 pages in all. You would go blind reading just the first chapter. 'I think this is just breathtaking,' Shaw says. 'The people who made

Matrices awaiting cleaning and cataloguing at the Type Archive

this would have been paid awful money and worked almost in the dark. And this is what the Type Archive is about. It's about the fact that human lives are here.'

Shaw is fond of saying that she has 'been in recession for two decades'. The Type Archive is a uniquely valuable institution, but investment is needed if she is ever to realize the blueprint on her desk, and open it to the public.

What would they find? A magical place – the history of writing in physical form, the uncelebrated hardware of our language. Everything here was once in clattering flow, all the 23,000 drawers of metal punches and matrices, hundreds of fonts in every size, all the flat-bed presses, all 600,000 copper letter patterns, all the keyboards and casting machines setting hot metal type, all the woodletter type collections and machines from the DeLittle company in York, all the steel history from Sheffield, all the hundredweights of artefacts that made the great libraries of the world. This is where it ended up when computers arrived. All quiet now.

The collection arrived here in the mid-1990s, and it took Momart, the fine art movers, seven weeks to bring in just one part of it from Surrey, and when they were done they said they'd be glad to get back to the Henry Moores again. Recent visitors included *Harry Potter* film people in search of inspiration and inky atmosphere, and a large team from Google, who came to see where their world began.

Sue Shaw gave them the brochures, exquisite hand-printed documents in black and red in Caslon and Gill Sans with perfect spacing and pilcrows (the traditional printers' mark that denotes a paragraph break or pause for thought, 'the backwards-facing P'). They tell of ambitious plans to open this vault not as a mausoleum but a place of training, where apprentices may come to learn the mechanical manufacture of type, a highly skilled manual endeavour. The first training manual, describing a process of facing, stamping, striking, lapping, coning, turning and side-milling for a 0.2" matrix, has already been produced, precise as its tools: 'Test first matrix depth of character impression using depth-testing micrometer machine No 60. Depth reading should be +0.0045" to 0.005". Check results with supervisor.'

The Type Archive's founder and director, Shaw is a combination of forceful pragmatist and proud elitist. In the pre-computer age she worked at Penguin, Chatto and Faber & Faber ('where we even made a book on compost look good'). She is still involved in fine printing, and a guided tour of the Type Museum may take in a book that took six years to prepare for Paul Mellon and the Roxburghe Club: a facsimile of the *Helmingham Herbal and Bestiary* from 1500, containing 150 illustrations of plants and animals real and imaginary, the display text in 24pt Stephenson Blake Caslon.

The names of other fonts may be found elsewhere in this archive in the bound records of Stephenson Blake, Britain's oldest and longest surviving typefounder in Sheffield and London – or it was until it shut for good in 2004 and sold the Sheffield site to be made into flats. In its heyday, which covered 1830 to 1970, it swallowed up the punches and matrices of the vast majority of British typefoundries stretching back to John Day in the sixteenth century, and encompassing hallowed designs and equipment from

Joseph Fry, the Caslon dynasty and William Thorowgood. Stephenson Blake manufactured typefaces for the world, and the names are regal, distant and grand: Ancient Black, Impact, Runnymede, Hogarth, Olympian, Monumental, Renaissance, Windsor. They even had a precursor of Comic Sans: Ribbonface Typewriter, created in 1894.

But it was a wonder that the company survived into the twentieth century. Stephenson Blake supplied the Gutenberg method of typecasting, a laborious hand-built process that had changed little in four hundred years. A punch was still hammered into a softer matrix, a matrix was still placed in a mould. Lead, antimony and tin was still poured in. In 1845 a New York typefounder named David Bruce Jr patented the pivotal caster, a small hot-metal machine that produced any amount of the same letter. And then, forty years later, Linn Boyd Benton invented the pantographic punchcutter in Milwaukee. This was an ingenious router that cut steel punches for metal type (it was swiftly adapted for wood type, too), and led directly to the invention of two American machines that changed not only the way type was made, but almost everything about the way type was consumed for the next eighty years.

The Linotype (1886) and Monotype (1897) systems of mechanical typesetting produced words on paper far more efficiently, cheaply and quickly than hand composition. Monotype machines cast single characters out of molten (hot) metal, while Linotype models produced solid bars or slugs containing more than 100 letters (hence line-o-type). Linotype text was faster to manipulate but harder and more wasteful to correct, and flourished primarily in large-scale newspaper composition, while Monotype found a home at book printers and local printshops throughout the world. New publishers and publications flourished, which went some way to offsetting the loss of hand-compositors' jobs. After Gutenberg, mechanical casting was the second great revolution in movable metal type, and it would be the last. Beyond it lay phototypesetting and laser printing, and the awakening of Silicon Valley.

Both Monotype and Linotype enjoyed staggeringly rapid growth, and initially they loathed and feared each other. In November 1895, *Black and White* magazine, which was still composed the old-fashioned way, ran a full-page advertisement for Linotype that warned printers off its rival and dismissed the 'completely untrue' statements that the Linotype system was not already the machine of

Revolutionary machines – Monotype (above) and Linotype (opposite) adverts from the 1890s

choice in the United States. The advert* listed more than 300 newspapers currently using the Linotype, from the *New York Herald* (which had fifty-two machines) to the *New York Times* (twenty-five machines), to the Gloversville Leader (one machine). 'The machines that are now being offered for sale in England … are regarded by the associated bodies of American newspaper owners as anachronisms, and it is because they can get no foothold in America that they are trying to establish themselves in England. They can only cause loss and disappointment to all concerned.' Too late: Monotype already had hundreds of orders for their machines, and soon it would be thousands.

Monotype, which was based in Salfords, Surrey, and grew so big that it needed its own railway station, also had another huge impact on the printing world: it transformed the design of fonts. Initially both companies relied on adapting

old faces to their new technology, although they soon found that their clients wanted more than Garamond and Bodoni. When the traditional American and European type foundries amalgamated to head off the new competition, it was the great variety and durability of their designs that saved them. But soon it would be Monotype setting the pace, not least after it hired Stanley Morison as typographical consultant and Beatrice Warde as publicity manager (the company employed an unusually large amount of skilled women).

Before Morison appeared, Monotype fonts were largely predictable and conservative – almost a third of the first fifty typefaces on offer were heavy German blackletters and the main consideration was taking popular fonts once used in hand composition and converting them for mechanical use. When Morison set to work in 1923, after stints in publishing, he too was concerned with the likes of Bembo and Baskerville, and their continued popularity today relied on Monotype's finesse in modifying serifs and weights not just to the mechanical casting, but also to new printing techniques and the characteristics of machine-made paper. But his greatest contribution was the commissioning

* The other side of the Linotype advertisement contained smaller notices for Carter's Little Liver Pills, Cuticura Skin Cure and Musgrave's Ulster Stoves ('as supplied to Prince Bismarck') in fonts that were wild and loose, each using a variety of faces, shouting at the reader like fairground barkers. From German blackletter to English grotesque to Parisian antique, the fonts were seldom suitable for the dubious products, the compositors seemingly choosing type at random in the dark. This disharmony wasn't resolved in the advertising world until the late 1920s, when marketing people slowly awoke to the early possibilities of branding and saw how type could say much beyond mere words. This process was abetted by the Monotype Super Caster, which made new large-size display letters cheaply, thus diminishing the practice of relying on old irregular fonts from an unsorted box.

and purchase of new designs. He stayed with Monotype throughout his modernization of *The Times* in the 1930s and his editorship of the *Times Literary Supplement* in the 1940s, and a Monotype specimen book from the late 1960s reflects the extent of his influence.

As well as Eric Gill's Gill Sans, Perpetua and Joanna, there is Albertus, new versions of Bell, Walbaum and Ehrhardt, and Lutetia, Spectrum, Emerson, Rockwell and Festival Titling. And then there is the most widely used of all – Morison's own classic font, **Times New Roman**, which he designed at Monotype for *The Times*. Although it is no longer used by *The Times* itself, the font rivals Helvetica and Univers for ubiquity. Thousands of books are still set in it each year and, rolled out with every version of Windows since 1992, it appears in millions of documents, emails and web pages.

Large portions of the twentieth century breathed through Monotype's fonts. Their impact was documented in the *Monotype Recorder*, *Monotype Bulletin* and *Monotype Newsletter*, each a vibrant combination of in house journal, trade notices and academic treatises. The articles emphasize the immense expertise that good typesetting required. It took seven years to become a fully qualified Monotype operator and in this time one developed a spatial awareness – a sense of light, length and the justification of a line of type – that modern computers still struggle to match. Without this, letters and words would be as lost as musical notes without bars.

Beatrice Warde contributed an essay to the *Recorder* called 'Recent Achievements in Bible Typography'. Should

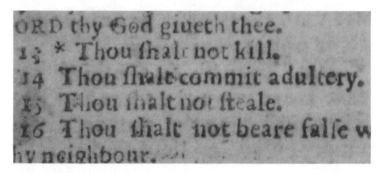

The worst typo of all time?

they have a single column or two? Set in Bembo or Van Dijck? One thing was for sure: no one wanted a repeat of Christopher Barker's Bible of 1631, which omitted the negative from the seventh commandment so that it read, 'Thou shalt commit adultery'.

In the 1940s there was an article about the old and new ways of learning to read, and how certain typefaces might assist. **Ehrhardt** from 1938 was reckoned particularly good. **Univers** and **Century Schoolbook** were clear and unconfusing too. In the 1950s there was the announcement of **Monotype Dante**, 'designed for printers by a printer'. The printer in question, Dr Giovanni Mardersteig, was not *only* a printer: he was also a scholarly editor who understood the gulf between designing a type and engraving it, and he possessed a treasured comprehension of 'the many subtle interrelationships between letterforms, without which no designer can draw types to combine perfectly into words'. Dante was just the most recent offering. There was a type for every occasion, and every month seemed to bring something new.

And then in June 1970 came a sinister notice in *Monotype Bulletin #81*: 'The general outlook for hot metal in the trade is bleak. The columns of the trade press are full of articles about filmsetting.' A new technology was approaching, but Monotype reckoned it would cope: they had the new Monophoto 600, a machine using Monotype modules, an early example of digital type. But beyond filmsetting there was something else, captured in the same edition: a photo of a temperature-controlled room dominated by huge cupboards of computers. The *Bulletin* reckoned that hot metal would merely be programmed by these white machines; they never saw them taking over.*

And so here they are, those redundant machines, in an old horse hospital in Lambeth – a priceless archive for those interested in tactile, precise and highly skilled methods of the past. There is the very first Monotype keyboard from 1897 (it looks just like a typewriter; the only other known example is in the Smithsonian). And here is its sister, a casting machine that ran on compressed air. There are a dozen more recent models that can be hooked up to laptops,

* The Monotype name nonetheless continues to be a dominant force in type design, though its focus has changed immeasurably since opening a Silicon Valley office in Palo Alto in 1991. There, Monotype licensed its fonts to Microsoft, Apple and Adobe, adapted for digital software formats. Its headquarters is now in Massachusetts, but it continues to run its UK operations from Salfords. It has incorporated both Linotype and the International Typeface Corporation (ITC), and in March 2010 it announced its Creative Companion Library, a cut-price deal for those wanting to start a new digital font library. This was a huge collection of fonts, all available in the latest OpenType format for all computer platforms: 2,433 typefaces in all, including Frutiger, Palatino and ITC Conduit. There was no Helvetica or many other desirables, but it was still quite a bargain at $4,999 for up to ten workstations using one printer. Professional fonts, once hand-drawn by scribes, then hand-cut and hand-tooled and toiled over for months, were now about $2 each.

the equivalent of the 1930s candlestick phone being plugged into fibre-optic cables. We miss these things – the old feel, the old look and the old smell, the old clunk, the use of our whole hand, not just the push-button part that wears away our fingerprints.

But the craft is not quite dead. The Type Museum occasionally calls in a couple of the old Monotype operators to demonstrate mastery of their machines for those who might offer financial backing for the renovations of both the building and the art, and establish an enticing experience for visitors and apprenticeships to keep the craft alive. Sue Shaw remains optimistic. 'Can there be anything more valuable?' she asks. 'And if there are no jobs at the end of it, that's not necessarily a reason not to do it. There's no jobs after reading poetry, either.'

And how best to make a wonderful book now? The craft of the Kelmscott Press, Golden Cockerell Press or Doves Press has not been lost – there are hundreds of small presses in the UK, Europe and the United States. One of the newest is White's Books, which in the spring of 2010 had just eight titles in its list, although as lists go it was a sound one: *Emma*, *Pride and Prejudice*, *Wuthering Heights*, *Treasure Island*, *Jane Eyre* and collections of Dickens, Shakespeare and Conan Doyle.

They are beautiful editions, and with their marker ribbon, coloured endpapers and clothbound jacket illustrations they feel like a product from a more considerate age. The person responsible for their appearance is David Pearson, who has worked extensively with Penguin, most famously on its

Keeping up traditions: typographic covers from Penguin's *Great Ideas* series. The designers are, clockwise from top left: Phil Baines, Catherine Dixon, Alistair Hall and David Pearson.

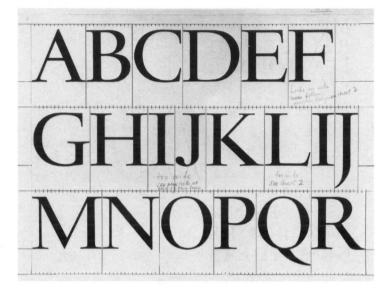

Jan van Krimpen's original drawings for Haarlemmer

Great Ideas series – the packaging of essays from Seneca to Orwell in slim paperbacks with great attention paid to the typography on the jackets.

These books, and the White's classics, are notable too for a tiny detail on the preliminary pages. Alongside the copyright details and name of the printers, we learn a little about the choice and size of type. The Penguins, for example, are credited as Monotype Dante. The crediting of a font is a disappearing feature these days, and a dispiriting absence. A random selection from the shelves at the London Library suggests the pattern emerged with the move to digital. Saul Bellow's *Humboldt's Gift* asserted that it was set in Baskerville, Philip Roth's *Portnoy's Complaint* appeared in Granjon; *Laughing Gas* by PG Wodehouse in Linotype Baskerville, while Graham Greene's *The Honorary Consul* was in Monotype Times. But recent hardbacks by Ian McEwan and Julian Barnes? We can only guess. The same goes for John Richardson's *Picasso* and Ian Kershaw's *Hitler* – big, important, illustrated books, but with type not considered worthy of acknowledgement.

For his White's classics, Pearson chose Monotype Haarlemmer, setting it '11 on 15' – 11 point type with a 4-point leading. The font is a modern interpretation of a serif conceived by Jan van Krimpen in the 1930s, its original production sidelined by the war. It has a tall X-height, creating a clean and airy appearance and achieving just the effect required for a modern take on a traditional text.

'The skill is creating a nice even consistency without any rivers or gaps,' Pearson explained in his office overlooking an outpost of Central Saint Martin's art school in Farringdon. 'You don't want unsightly line breaks or excessive white space, and as few hyphens as possible. Setting a book can be a very mundane boring process, day after day after day – and you'll only hear about it if it's done badly.'

Pearson says he would have liked to have used Monotype Dante for his White's Books – 'there's no contest with 10 on 13 Monotype Dante for hot metal' – but his experience with the Penguin *Great Ideas* project taught him that the digital version will never look as good. 'And when you have a set of books stretching on in front of you and you have to choose one typeface, you have to know it can handle any idiosyncrasy in the text. Your choice may often come down to "Has it got a small caps italic?" So few of them do. You don't want to fudge that small caps italic or the whole thing is just shot to pieces.'

There is another rare feature that places his books among the remnants of a type museum – the setting of a catchword at the bottom of the right-hand page. This is a preview of the first word on the next page, an aid intended to smooth the flow when books are read aloud. 'It's an embellishment,' Pearson says, 'but it shows care. It reaffirms the tradition of the book as a valuable and desirable object.'

Sabon

This book – the main chapters and also this very paragraph that you are reading – is set in Sabon. It is not the most beautiful type in the world, nor the most original or arresting. It is, however, considered one of the most readable of all book fonts; and it is one of the most historically significant.

Sabon was developed in the early 1960s for a group of German printers who were grumbling about the lack of a 'harmonized' or uniform font that would look the same whether set by hand or on a Monotype or Linotype machine. They were quite specific about the sort of font that might fit the bill, rejecting the modern and fashionable in favour of solid sixteenth-century tradition – something modelled on Garamond and Granjon. They also wanted the new font to be five per cent narrower than their existing Monotype Garamond, in order to save space and money.

The man chosen for this task was Jan Tschichold, a Leipzig-born typographer, who in the 1920s had devised a 'universal alphabet' for German, cleaning up its non-phonetic spellings and advocating the replacement of the jumble of fonts with a simple sans serif. He was a modernist, an enthusiast for the Bauhaus, who had been arrested by the Gestapo for communist sympathies before fleeing Nazi Germany for Switzerland. And after the war, from 1947 to 1949, he played a hugely significant role in British book design, creating timeless modern layouts and fonts for Penguin books.

Tschichold had by this time entirely changed his mind over the 'single font' idea for German, dismissing his idea as 'juvenile', and now advocated classical typefaces as the most legible. For the German printers, he therefore crafted a font that modernized the classics and honed each letter's fine details, particularly the evenness of the serifs. In doing so, he took careful account of the added weight needed to form a strong impression on modern paper, the mechanized machines subtly 'kissing' the surface with ink rather than stamping or rolling it.

Tschichold's drawings for Sabon

The result was Sabon, which took its name from Jacques Sabon, the owner of a sixteenth-century type foundry in Frankfurt that issued the first-known type specimen book. The new typeface was issued jointly by Germany's three main type foundries (Linotype, Monotype and Stempel) and became hugely popular in book and magazine printing. It remains a favourite among the discerning and it looks particularly good the bigger you use it, which is why magazines like *Vogue* and *Esquire* use a slightly modified version of it for headlines.

Its popularity and purpose was perhaps best defined by Tschichold himself, in his treatise *Die Neue Typographie*:

> The essence of the New Typography is Clarity. This puts it into deliberate opposition to the old typography whose aim was 'beauty' and whose clarity did not attain the high level we require today. This utmost clarity is necessary today because of the manifold claims for our attention made by the extraordinary amount of print, which demands the greatest economy of expression.

He was writing in 1928.

Fonts, like life, are governed by rules. It's not necessarily a bad thing, being told to sit up straight and not covet thy neighbour's ox, and we'd all be lost without i before e except after c. But to what extent do rules stifle individuality and creativity? What happens to the minds of a million first-year art students when faced with the task of designing a great new typeface? They too are contained by parameters, creativity blocked in like a palette knife shaping wet cement.

The most instinctive designers (the true artists) will know what works and what to discard. But the novice is hampered by the weight of history and the dead grey hand of the instruction manual. For many of the rules of type are really rules of typography, bound up not just with their appearance but with their use on a page; useful on their own, they can be destructive in combination.

To demonstrate how unappealing and under-considered these rules can be, the writer Paul Felton created an ingenious and beautiful book. Turn it one way and you get *The Ten Commandments of Typography*; turn it round and shift its axis, and it becomes *Type Heresy*. To support each side (Good v Evil), Felton comes up with a list of 'Twelve Disciples of Type', including Paul Renner and Eric Gill, and pits against them his own, more anarchic design heroes ('the Fallen Angels of Typography').

Here are the rules, as Felton considers God intended them:

1. Thou shalt not apply more than three typefaces in a document.
2. Thou shalt lay headlines large and at the top of the page.
3. Thou shalt employ no other type size than 8pt to 10pt for body copy.
4. Remember that a typeface that is not legible is not truly a typeface.
5. Honour thy kerning, so that white space becomes visually equalized between characters.
6. Thou shalt lay stress discreetly upon elements within text.
7. Thou shalt not use only capitals when setting vast body copy.
8. Thou shalt always align letters and words on a baseline.

9. Thou shalt use flush-left, ragged-right
type alignment.
10. Thou shalt not make lines too short
or too long.

Flipping the book over, Felton kicks off the case for heresy himself, listing the twenty-four different fonts he has chosen for the book, before inviting the Fallen Angels to debunk each rule. There's a particularly nice line against the Seventh Commandment: 'CAPITALISED TEXT MAY MAKE MORE OF A DEMAND ON THE READER BUT WHAT THE HELL IS WRONG WITH THAT?'

In the introduction to the dark side, one of the fallen angels, Jonathan Barnbrook, creator of the Mason and Priori font families, observes that his old tutors at art school tried to instill rules merely to stop their students having too much fun. 'Typography truly reflects the whole of human life,' he maintains, 'and it changes with each generation. It may well be the most direct visual representation of the tone of voice with which we express the spirit of the time.'

There is a long history of type instruction and discussion, a tradition stretching as far back as Aldus Manutius in the sixteenth century. In fact, there seems to be something about type design that lends itself to philosophizing.

The approaches can be fundamental and rhetorical: 'I AM TYPE!' Frederic Goudy declared in 1931. 'Through me, Socrates and Plato, Chaucer and the bards become your faithful friends who ever surround and minister to you. I am the leaden army that conquers the world.' They

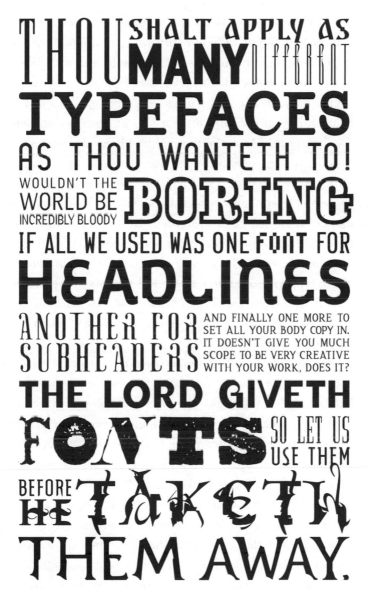

THOU SHALT APPLY AS MANY DIFFERENT TYPEFACES AS THOU WANTETH TO! WOULDN'T THE WORLD BE INCREDIBLY BLOODY BORING IF ALL WE USED WAS ONE FONT FOR HEADLINES ANOTHER FOR SUBHEADERS AND FINALLY ONE MORE TO SET ALL YOUR BODY COPY IN. IT DOESN'T GIVE YOU MUCH SCOPE TO BE VERY CREATIVE WITH YOUR WORK, DOES IT? THE LORD GIVETH FONTS SO LET US USE THEM BEFORE HE TAKETH THEM AWAY.

Dark Satanic stuff – Paul Felton's plea for heresy

can be iconoclastic: 'By all means break the rules,' implored Robert Bringhurst in *The Elements of Typographic Style*, 'and break them beautifully, deliberately, and well. That is one of the ends for which they exist.' Or they can be poetic: 'Type is like music in having its own beauty, and in being beautiful as an accompaniment and interpretation,' wrote the printer JH Mason in the middle of the last century.

More often, especially in our Internet age, they are vituperative. 'There's no legitimate typographic reason to create an alphabet which looks like it leaked out of a diaper,' reasoned Peter Fraterdeus in the *AIGA Journal of Graphic Design* in 1996. (He was talking specifically about 'degenerate' type, the sort made by the amateur mucking about with Fontographer software.) Or this observation on digital type from the design critic Paul Hayden Duensing: 'Digitizing [the seventeenth-century typeface] Janson is like playing Bach on synthesizer.'

The typographic rulebooks began appearing in swift succession from the 1920s, the decade when we thought we had a handle on things. The type technologies were fairly settled – mechanized hot metal machines set everything in the western world from the grandest newspapers to the plainest calling card. But it was a world that seemed to get smaller each time you looked at it. Everything in the first quarter of the twentieth century seemed to have a code and regulation that guaranteed consistency and good form, but frowned upon deviation and shunned innovation. A new recruit to the fold found it almost impossible to market a new typeface until they had spent several decades theorizing about its forerunners. In this regard, type was like painting and architecture: an elitism prevailed, and what you produced was only half the story, and what you said about it counted just as much.

Working on his redesign of *The Times*, Stanley Morison advanced conservative justifications for holding back what he perceived as a worrying trend towards untutored individualism. The type designer and printer, he said, were engaged principally to give the public what they're used to. 'No printer should say, I am an artist ... I will create my own letter forms." The good type designer ... realizes that, for a new fount to be successful, it has to be so good that only very few recognize its novelty. If my friends think that the tail of my lower-case r or the lip of my lower-case e is rather jolly, you may know that the fount would have been better had neither been made.'

You can see exactly that philosophy at work in Morison's creation of Times New Roman for *The Times* – a serif font modelled on a sixteenth-century face from the Plantin-Moretus Foundry in Antwerp, adapted to maximize its legibility and

"THE TIMES" IN NEW TYPE

HOW THE CHANGE WAS MADE

The change of type completed with this morning's issue of *The Times* has involved one of the biggest undertakings ever accomplished in a newspaper office. More than two years have been devoted to designing and cutting the type characters for ultimate use in the two systems of mechanical composition used on *The Times*—linotype and monotype. To equip the battery of linotype (including inter-

"THE TIMES"

LAST DAY OF THE OLD TYPE

MONDAY'S CHANGES

The Times appears to-day for the last time in the type to which the present generation has grown accustomed.

On Monday the changes already announced in the text and the main title will be made. Their object is to secure greater legibility on every page and to give the reader a type which will respond to every

Morison's Times makeover

economic use of space. If we had been present at the meetings at which his work was proposed, we would have heard a man explaining how well his type worked at very small sizes in compact columns; it was a tight serif but not in the least fancy; it had short ascenders and descenders; its capitals were contained and unobtrusive.

It was one of the most successful type designs in history – used unchanged by *The Times* for the next forty years, and adopted worldwide. And Morison's principles apply equally to Matthew Carter's Georgia, which he designed as a screen font for Microsoft (it is the serif companion to Verdana), as a modern take on Morison's Times New Roman.

Morison was not only a master craftsman, he was also one of Britain's leading historians of type. But he lived in an age when news still travelled slowly. The modernizing and pioneering influences of Paul Renner and Jan Tschichold in Germany had clearly not yet been felt at Printing House Square, or perhaps they had been repelled along with the politically objectionable Italian Futurists and Russian Constructivists. But the waves lapping in from Europe would soon have a bracing effect, bringing onshore such things as asymmetrical type and diagonally cut lines.

In mid-October 2004, the highly regarded printer, designer and writer Sebastian Carter delivered the Beatrice Warde Memorial Lecture at the St Bride Institute. It had been seventy-four years since Warde had herself delivered her famous talk, and Carter's subject was not too dissimilar, given that it was part of a three-day symposium entitled 'Bad Type'.

Times New Roman – a most enduring font

Georgia – not so different, great on screen

Principled typefaces – Morison's Times New Roman and
Matthew Carter's Georgia

This was the rulebook in reverse, or white on black. Carter began by running through several notable instruction manuals on type and typography, which had 'a way of imposing solutions and limiting choices'. He discussed the value of the jobs undertaken by small presses and extolled the worth of ephemera. Carter himself ran the small Rampant Lions Press in Cambridge, where he (and his father, Will, before him) produced exquisite work. But he also championed the not-such-a-great-job, the pieces of design and printing that didn't turn out to be beautiful or clear, merely interesting. He illustrated his talk with some items that were 'pretty cruddy', and suggested that these too had a place in our world. 'I would not want to live in a world of exclusively good design at the bus-ticket level,' he said.

Carter was preceded onto the platform by Nigel Bents, a senior lecturer at Chelsea College of Art and Design, who pronounced that he had had enough of perfect type, wrought according to perfect rules. In its place he proposed a love letter to disaster. 'What we need is a manifesto,' he told his audience of designers, 'set diagonally and vertically, all script caps with soft shadows, outlined and underlined, with poor punctuation and hundreds of hyphens, stretched to the edge and cropped at the sides, printed in yellow on day-glo paper, trimmed badly and poorly presented.'

Thus armed, 'the designers of tomorrow will not look back; we give them the chance to fail abjectly and completely; they're all in the typographic gutter and some of them are looking at their scars.' The result, of course, would bring forth more failure, but also types of originality and brilliance. 'We could become a nation of typographic genii through a litany of design atrocities,' Bents reasoned.

But is that what we've got now? Does the type you see around you enhance your day? A survey of manifestos and guide books suggests that our hands can only be held so much, and for the rest we must trust to inspiration. The only intractable, invincible basic rules of good type? Make it interesting, make it beautiful, and bring out both its humanity and its soul. Make it tasteful and witty and apt. And readable.

Or change your name to Neville Brody. If you were Neville Brody you could join a London-based magazine called *The Face* in 1981 and transform its rather predictable design to such a degree that your impact would be felt not just on the look of magazines but on books, music, and many aspects of commercial product design for decades to come. If you were Neville Brody you could set up a design business called Research Studios with offices in five countries and rework the retail look of high-end fashion and perfume brands, and take up the post of head of Communication Art & Design at the Royal College of Art. You could give your typefaces monumental names like Typeface Four or Typeface Six and you could continue to wear a ponytail long after everyone else in the design world apart from Matthew Carter had been ridiculed into chopping theirs off.

Brody studied at the London College of Printing in the late 1970s, where he fell under the spell of punk and the possibilities of non-conformity, and where he was almost thrown out for designing a stamp with the Queen's head placed sideways. This was not just the punk of the Sex Pistols and their designer Jamie Reid's scissorly disrespect for old typography, but also the anarchy of his hero Alexander Rodchenko, who suggested that creativity was simply the force that people who made rules disapproved of.

The Eighties writ large – Neville Brody's trademark covers for *The Face*

Brody found his first expression in record sleeves, learning from Barney Bubbles at Stiff Records and Al McDowell at the design studio Rocking Russian. His work at *The Face* pushed, pulled, squeezed and bent type as it explored the edge between structure and legibility, and it sat well alongside the magazine's unusual use of Futura, Gill Sans Bold Condensed and Albertus. The wild geometry of his designs originated in the traditional way (drawing and cutting out shapes, working with Letraset and copiers) but it was the

boldness of his display that shook people – text occupying an entire page, the overlapping of type and a crashing of styles, the way the word 'contents' would gradually disintegrate across five monthly issues. He disliked the restrictions suggested by Beatrice Warde and Jan Tschichold, and he would try anything to shake off their suffocating influence.

By the time Brody got to work on *Arena* magazine in 1986 and the Victoria and Albert Museum displayed his typography two years later, his daring visual jokes and eagerness to confound had entered the consciousness

Contents graphic from *The Face*, 1984.

of graphic design students throughout the world. His embrace of digital possibilities continued to produce stunning fonts – from his Futura-style **Insignia** and fluid **Blur** in the early 1990s to his hard-edged Peace in 2009 – and they were often accompanied (in Brody's mind at least) by a weighty emotional or political message.

To hear Brody address his adoring students today – at London's Design Museum in the shadow of London Bridge – is to realize how little his worldview has changed. At fifty-two he still carries a fizzing resentment towards conformity, and expresses the hope that the economic crisis will usher forth a comparable cultural rebellion to the one that fired him thirty years before. 'Where is the language of protest now?' he asks. 'We have been led to believe that culture was only there as a financial opportunity.' He talks about danger and originality as the screen behind him flashes images from Man Ray and the Factory Records designer Peter Saville.

Brody conducts a swift slide show of his recent hits: the titles for the Michael Mann film *Public Enemies*, recent designs for *Wallpaper** and the typography magazine *Fuse*, a wall of surveillance cameras for his Freedom Space downstairs in the London Design Museum's Super Contemporary show. He pauses at an image of *The Times* from the nineteenth century, comparing it to his own redesign of the paper in 2006. He said he intended to give it greater clarity and energy, and one of his tools was new type – 8.5pt Times Classic for the main text and Obama's campaign face **Gotham** for the more compressed sans serif headlines.

The paper was following a trend: newspapers looking more like their web pages. The previous year the *Guardian* had also changed its type, from a mix of Helvetica, Miller and Garamond to its own Guardian Egyptian, a versatile and gentle font family comprising ninety-six variants designed by Paul Barnes and Christian Schwartz to accompany the paper's move to a smaller format.

The key, Brody said, in a strange echo of Morison, was 'to change a newspaper entirely, but to make sure no one noticed. Our main focus was on articulation, so the layout people could use each page as theatre. When we first showed it to focus groups they didn't notice it had changed, but when we told them it had changed, they hated it.'

Before he adjourned for a drink, Brody told his students that he was concerned about the genericism of our culture. 'Everywhere you go has similar spaces and signs,' he said. 'As designers we are complicit in this – we have to look for new ways forward. It's all about words that we don't use any more, like revolution and progress.' But there were limitations to his vision, an ambition sapped by studio bills, staff wages and the need to think deeply about branding possibilities for multinational clients pushing luxury products.

As for the Brody brand itself, the iconoclast still finds his purest refuge in type. His font designs of 2010 were called Buffalo and Popaganda, huge and beautiful architectural slabs of ink that clamber over each other in the fashionable magazines, always challenging and arresting, never content just to sit there and tell a story.

The Interrobang

The Interrobang is not a font – just a single character. Yet it is so powerful a symbol, and such a flawed and original concept, that it deserves a place alongside the most adventurous typographic innovations of the last century. It is an exclamation mark and question mark combined, a ligature looping the curve of the interrogation with the downward force of the expletive (which compositors and printers have traditionally called a bang). When they meld, they need only one round point at their base.

The Interrobang has its roots in 1960s advertising. The New York ad executive Martin Spekter was looking for a way to express astonishment, and disliked the clumsy combination of ?! when he wanted to say things like 'How much?!?!' and 'You're not serious?!' But when he expressed his frustration in a type magazine he only had the idea for it, not the name. Readers suggested the Exclamaquest and the QuizDing, before the Interrobang was chosen.

The new symbol had rapid appeal, provoking an article in the *Wall Street Journal* and inspiring Remington and IBM to offer additional keyboard keys. Its success was shortlived, however, perhaps because people liked the incredulity of emphasizing 'what the ****?!?!??!!' with lots of punctuation, and perhaps because the Interrobang could be ugly. You can find it in Microsoft Word Wingdings 2, and there are versions for Calibri and Helvetica and Palatino. At small sizes ‽ just looks a mess, as confused as the expression it conveys. And there was another reason it failed to last. We find it very hard to accept a new type mark, particularly one as forceful as this. An <u>underscore</u> is just about acceptable, as is the ™ symbol, and even the ^ sitting above the 6 on your keyboard (it is known as the *asciicircum* or *caret*). But the Interrobang – you're kidding right‽ The Interrobang is truly the Esperanto of fonts.

The one symbol that does buck the trend – although since email appeared in the 1980s we've not had much choice – is the 'at' (@) sign. The @ can be varied substantially to suit any typeface but it always looks technical, or as if it's trying to sell you something. Yet despite its current usage, the @ is not a product of the digital age, and may be almost as old as the ampersand. It had been associated with trade for many centuries, known as an *amphora* or jar, a unit of measurement. Most countries have their own term for it, often linked to food (in Hebrew it is *shtrudl*, meaning strudel, in Czech it is *zavinac* or rollmop herring) or to cute animals (*Affenschwanz* or monkey's tail in German, *grisehale* or pig's tail in Danish, *sobaka* or dog in Russian), or to both (*escargot* in French).

THE SERIF OF LIVERPOOL

19

Backstage in Boston, two hours before the gig, Paul McCartney is doing what he does best – reliving the glory days. It is August 2009. He has just soundchecked at Fenway Park, home of the Boston Red Sox, where, in front of an audience of eighty, he played songs he remembered from the Cavern Club and Abbey Road. 'And this is a new one,' he announced, as he began singing 'Yesterday'.

His backstage trailer looks like a Middle Eastern souk – rugs on the walls, rich embroidery, sweet candles burning on low tables. His girlfriend, Nancy Shevell, is preparing iced tea in a large wine glass, and McCartney is sitting with his feet curled under him on a sofa. His dyed brown hair is not as unnerving in reality as it can appear in photographs.

It is 2009 and he is sixty-seven, and a visitor to his lair might reasonably expect that he had long ago exhausted his stock of new Beatles stories, and his enthusiasm for telling them. But this is not the case. As so often with people of retirement age, yesterday is a little fuzzy but sixty years ago is sharper than ever, and he begins with a story of family holidays.

'When I was a kid, I went with my parents and my brother to Butlins Holiday Camp at Pwllheli. I had a vision ... what do you call it? An epiphany. I was by the swimming pool, and we were such a funny family, a little bit Alan Bennett. From a door in one of the buildings, I see four guys walk out in a line. They were all dressed the same. They all had grey crew-neck sweaters, tartan twat hats, tartan shorts, and a rolled white towel under their arm. I thought, "Holy shit!" Then I went to see them in the talent show, and they wore grey zoot suits, and they were from Gateshead, and they won. And I totally remember that. So when we came to be the Beatles, I said, "You know what?" and I told everyone about this epiphany. And so we ended up in suits and we all wore the same.'

So the look wasn't Brian Epstein's idea?

'I don't think it was.'

McCartney said he had always been fascinated by the appearance of things. A few weeks after his Boston show, his old band would make their first appearance in a video game, *The Beatles: Rockband*, which involves playing along to Beatles songs on plastic instruments and scoring points for how well you can strum with George or keep pace with Ringo. The game was being packaged with huge posters

The Beatles – boastful B, dropped T. Could be a band to watch

showing the band around the time of *A Hard Day's Night*. The font used to display the band's name looks like the one the band used at the time: thick black letters, small spiky serifs, the large boastful B at the start, that long T that extends below the baseline of the other capitals.

This was the logo-type that Ringo pounded behind on his bass drum skin when they played Shea Stadium in August 1965, the one that came up for auction at Sotheby's in August 1989, the logo that attached itself to most of the repackaging and merchandizing after their split. The video game designers have adapted it slightly for the drumkit that comes with their game: the B is taller, the counter space in the B and A is larger, and the bottom curl on the S has lost its serif and instead snakes devilishly towards a fine point.

'It wasn't a typeface,' McCartney says. 'I think I drew it when I was at school. I used to sit around endlessly with notebooks, drawing Elvis, drawing guitars, drawing logos, drawing my signature. At that sort of time we were starting the Beatles and I think in my drawings I hit upon the idea of having the T long. It's not going to do me any good to really claim that, but it's quite possible.' Others have also claimed credit – Ivor Arbiter, the London drum shop owner who claims to have designed it for £5, and sign painter Eddie Stokes who worked for Arbiter painting drum skins in his lunch hour. Whoever *was* responsible, it seems likely that the main subconscious influence on the look of the letters came from Goudy Old Style – which would place the nameplate of the most famous English pop group of all time firmly in the heritage of early twentieth-century America.

McCartney is more certain about the logo that came after. 'The Wings one was me,' he says. 'Do you remember Tommy Walls? Walls Ice Cream had a strip in *The Eagle* comic, the posh comic. I loved that arriving at my house. One of the characters was called Tommy Walls, he had adventures every week, and the Lucky Walls sign was [he puts his two hands together to form a W]. Linda encouraged the fans to do it, and the fans now will do that when we do a Wings song. I think I do have a branding brain. I would appreciate it when I saw an amazing logo. When I saw the Stones tongue I'd think, "Oh yeah – got that right"'.

Logotypes and brand marks, of course, are not the same as fonts, although they may soon become them. One can download a whole alphabet modelled on the Beatles logo (or their Magical Mystery Tour writing, or Lennon's handwriting) and if you use the letters to spell, say, **THE SMITHS** or **COLDPLAY**, it can be rather unnerving.

You can also get FLOYDIAN, a font 'created as a tribute' to Pink Floyd (resembling the scratchy letters drawn by Gerald Scarfe for THE WALL album) and **Zeppelin II**, 'a musical font that resembles one of the logos of the famous rock band', or GORILLAZ, modelled on the lettering created by Jamie Hewlett for Damon Albarn's cartoon band.*

The Beatles: Rock Band video game was released on the same day as the newly mastered and repackaged versions of all the albums, and spreading all the sleeves in a line provides an informative lesson in how, when it came to type, the most original and experimental band and their designers often used the fonts that just seemed to be knocking about. There's a heavy Letraset-application of sans serif on *Revolver,* embossed Helvetica for the *White Album*, a Univers type for the back of *Abbey Road* (reflecting the London street names in this style), a shaded, mildly psychedelic choice for the *Red* and *Blue* compilations.

---

* There are also several professionally made fonts with music-associated names that have no trademarked link with a band or its music: Achtung Baby, designed by John Roshell and Richard Starkins, in 1999; Acid Queen (Jackson Tan Tzun Tat, 1996); Tiger Rag (John Viner, 1989); Get Back (Pietervan Rosmalen, 1999).

There were notable exceptions, not least the bulbous psychedelia of *Yellow Submarine* designed to look like an underwater LSD trip, and the hand-drawn nameplate of *Rubber Soul* from 1965 that evoked the mindbending graphics of the underground magazines of the day. The lettering artist Charles Front received twenty-five guineas (£26.25) for his Rubber Soul letters – inspired by the idea of rubber pulled downwards by gravity. In 2008 he put the original artwork up for sale at Bonhams; it went for £9,600.

These days, a musical product with the ambition of the Beatles would never leave the management office without careful consideration of type. Despite McCartney's early school doodlings, his group didn't have a nameplate until several years into their career. Most artists now have a font that defines their style from the beginning, and even if they never went to art school they appear type-savvy. Some even sing about fonts.

Lily Allen went for an apocalyptic face for her debut album *Alright, Still*, all irregular jagged sizes and modular spacing, but then used type itself as the main image on the cover of her follow-up, *It's Not Me, It's You*, leaning back on a huge slab-serif L as if it was a lounge chair (actually she looks a little crammed in and uncomfortable). Sometimes personalization tries too hard. The use of handwriting – nicely illustrated on the same Lily Allen cover – seems to say, 'I'm just like you even though I'm famous and wealthy now.'

Often it's just better to be apart and extreme. Amy Winehouse's debut album *Frank* featured her name in a sharp angular sans serif that overlapped the title. But her diva image was far better suited to the glamour of the 1930s deco lettering on her follow-up *Back To Black*. This custom-made type has fine Gill Sans-style capitals at its root,

fattened up by a barcode of vertical stripes and bookended by another thicker line. The letters are loaded with historical significance, but the precise pedigree is hazy: an Atlantic ocean liner perhaps, or a poster announcing a new Gershwin show.

The *Back To Black* font has notable antecedents: the Atlas face designed by KH Schaefer and issued by Francaise type foundry in 1933 (also known as Fatima), and Ondina, designed by K Kranke for the Schriftguss foundry in 1935. It works for Winehouse not just because it reflects her voice, which is something from a former and smokier age, but because it's a shortcut to brand recognition. You need just see the A to recognize the product, the way you just need the long T to recognize the Beatles.

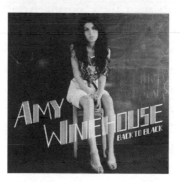

In a crowded field, like pop music, personality can be key. To emphasize the idea that Coco Sumner is not just the daughter of Sting and Trudie Styler, but a credible performer

Personal touch – handwriting as font

in her own right, her pop band I Blame Coco promotes itself with a script typeface specifically based on her handwriting. Vampire Weekend, the hot college band of 2010, were so keen to associate themselves with modernist and experimental **Futura Bold** that they not only used it big on their breakthrough album **CONTRA** but also mention the font in their song 'Holiday', about a girl who has never seen the word 'bombs' written 'in ninety-six-point Futura'.

The music world has always had an intimate relationship with the type world, but never has it been so keen to emphasize the fact. Kylie Minogue features in a song by Towa Tei called 'German Bold Italic', while the Boston band the Grace Period has recorded a song called 'Boring Arial Layout' (which, on their album *Dynasty*, followed a track called 'How To Get Ahead In Advertising'). And there are at least two that would have Stanley Morison turning in his grave: 'Times New Roman' by the Applicants, and 'Times New Romance' by Monochrome.

One suspects that a fair number of these bands have been influenced by the work of Peter Saville, whose Factory Records work for Joy Division/New Order defined the use

Idiosyncratic type combo – the woodblock is taken from a series of decorative alphabets by Louis John Pouchée, who ran a London type foundry in the 1820s

of type on album covers through the 1980s. Saville is more art director than typographer but customized the fonts for his projects and put them centre stage. And it is hard to resist the typographic combination on his cover of Pulp's *We Love Life*, which combines a Victorian woodblock Fat Face with a Dymo label.

But for the most recognizable letters in modern music we should look beyond a band or its record sleeve to a man driving along in an open-top car towards his home in Oakland California. This is Jim Parkinson, baseball cap and goatee beard, designer of such fonts as Jimbo, Balboa, Mojo and Modesto, graphic embodiments of the Californian dream. Parkinson's life is like a Doobie Brothers song, a band for whom he has designed album covers. He likes wild type, fairground type, type that speaks of the more indulgent and liberated things in life, including loud rock music and youthful rebellion. Now approaching seventy, he designs the sort of type children would design given half a chance.

Parkinson grew up in Richmond, California, and as a child used to visit an elderly lettering artist who drew fancy certificates commemorating big achievements with loopy capitals. After art school he landed a job at Hallmark cards in Kansas, where he worked on fonts that were made to look like handwriting. He gave them names at random: Cheap Thrills, Horsey, Punk. 'I named one of them "I Don't Know", just so I could say it when someone asked me what it was called.'

He thinks he must have made fifty or sixty different styles, drawing freehand pen and ink on tissue paper. He showed me one with this (handwritten) legend:

*Though we think of our friends
many times through the year
And wish them happiness too
It's especially pleasant
when Christmas is here
To remember and say that we do.
Merry Christmas.*

It was while he was creating these Hallmark fonts* that Parkinson read about the counter-culture in San Francisco. He moved back to California and took all the work he could get: posters for The New Riders of the Purple Sage, potato chip packets, type for Creedence Clearwater Revival and one for The Ringling Bros and Barnum & Bailey Circus that survived for twenty years.

On his more buttoned-down, bill-paying days, Parkinson has updated mastheads (or, strictly speaking, 'nameplates') for the likes of the *Wall Street Journal*, *Esquire*, *Newsweek* and the *Los Angeles Times* – many of them classic English blackletters that needed to be moved on a century. But his most famous and recognizable lettering adorns the masthead for a magazine that once defined a generation: *Rolling Stone*. This is a blocky but fluid type with 3-D shading, the sort one might attempt when doodling. The R loops like a sustained guitar note, its tail curling beneath the o to reach the l, while the lower bowl of the g smirks as it fuses with the S. It is strong, clean and as perennially appealing as a well-wrapped tube of sweets. One letter alone identifies it on the news stand, and it can stand any amount of being obscured by the cover stars' heads. 'I used to dismiss it,' Jim Parkinson says, 'telling people I had also done a lot of other things. But now I embrace it.'

There are few more redolent or potent graphic images of the Sixties, even if Parkinson only got to work on it in 1977.

* Some of Parkinson's early work is packaged in the fonts selection provided with Hallmark Card Studio 2010 Deluxe, a software package that enables you to make cards at home. There are 10,000+ card designs, 7,500 sentiments, and a surprisingly wide-ranging selection of typefaces, slanted towards script fonts with ill-fitting names (CarmineTango, Caslon AntT, Starbabe HMK).

'This is the first one,' he says, consulting a book of Rolling Stone covers in his studio. It was drawn by psychedelic-poster artist Rick Griffin, who received $75 for something he considered merely a sketch. Jann Wenner, the magazine's editor, decided there wasn't enough time to refine it; the first masthead appeared over a picture of John Lennon in army garb and a story about the missing money from the Monterey pop festival. It was cleaned up over the years, most notably

Rick Griffin's original *Rolling Stone* masthead

by John Pistilli, designer of the Didot-style Pistilli Roman, who added more flourishes and fanciful balls to the foot of many letters. Parkinson was asked to change it for the 10th anniversary issue in 1977 (the cover image was simply a giant Parkinson-shaded X).

Parkinson's redrawn *Rolling Stone* masthead – you need no more than the R to recognize it

The designer flicks through more changes, stopping at a cover from January 1981, the first where the lettering on the masthead is joined up. 'It was a big change, but nobody noticed,' he says. This was because readers were concentrating on the photo beneath it, by Annie Leibovitz, of a naked John Lennon curled up around a clothed Yoko, the issue that marked his murder.

It was rare at that time for a magazine to have custom typefaces for its entire editorial content, but the designer Roger Black asked Parkinson to do those as well. The family was inspired by fifteenth-century Italian serifs; Parkinson calls them 'Nicolas Jenson on acid', although there is also a lot of Cochin, a popular 1913 font, in there. When the type family was digitized in the 1990s, the attempts to register it as Rolling Stone were blocked for copyright reasons connected with the band. So they called it Parkinson. There are ten styles and weights – from Parkinson Roman to **Parkinson Condensed Bold**.

The walls of Parkinson's home studio provide a checklist of the classic inspirations of American type. His shelves hold books on Caslon and German gothics, script types suggested by the Speedball pen company, and specimen books from the Bruce New York type foundry from 1882, Stephenson Blake from 1926, and Letraset from the 1970s. Nearby there are physical letters – U, F, C and K – that once graced a theatre marquee, which he found irresistible.

'Too often ideas get lost because type insinuates itself between the reader and the idea,' Parkinson says. 'It's not all about simplicity, because you have to always keep things interesting, but the type must never be allowed to become too important. Letters evolve by trial and error – by public scrutiny, by standing the test of time. A lot of designers today don't have the patience for that.'

Fontbreak

Vendôme

Sometimes you just need a type that says Pleasure, possibly in French. A font for a luxury watch, maybe, or a restaurant. The name you need is Vendôme – a font designed in 1952 by a stage designer, François Ganeau, at Fonderie Olive, the foundry that also gave us **BANCO** and **Antique Olive**.

The face may have been named after Place Vendôme in Paris or perhaps the town along the Loire, but one thing is certain: it had to take a circumflex. Vendôme is as French as a baguette, proud and dismissive. It is modelled on the sixteenth- and seventeenth-century types by Claude Garamond and Jean Jannon, but is hardly respectful of them, with its serifs of irregular lengths in the same letter (the K, L, M and N have some serifs of equal width, some shorter on the left and some on the right).

Ganeau was a sculptor and theatre designer, and the tactile, three-dimensional element is clearly evident in his type. It looks as if it has been hurriedly cut out of black paper with no attempt to clean it up, and the result, especially in its bold and extra bold version, is a delightful statement of freedom. If you don't want a corny old art deco sign for your mid-market bistro or café, you use Vendôme and a stylish clientele will rush to sit beneath it.

'It's gorgeous,' says the book designer David Pearson. 'Really sculptural and sensual. I'd like to use it more than I do. But you hardly see it in Britain. In France it is so overused that it's been devalued, like Helvetica.' When Pearson was asked to select one perfect letterform, he picked the Vendôme Bold C, particularly keen on the distortion that called to mind 'ill-fitting corsets' and a tool that removes staples. He called Vendôme his mistress. 'Baskerville is my default, but sometimes you just have to break free.'

$$V_E{}^N{}D^O{}_M{}^E$$

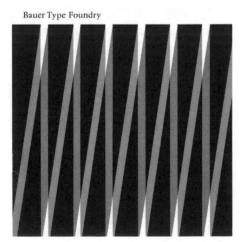

Bauer Type Foundry

Marketing for Vendôme from the Bauer Type Foundry

Fox, Gloves

20

Still, after all these years, *the quick brown fox jumps over the lazy dog*. This is a pangram, a phrase containing all the letters of the alphabet, and it endures, like the Alphabet Song in *Sesame Street*, for the simple reason that the phrase is rare, and no one has yet been able to think of a better one. As such, it is instantly familiar to anyone in the type world – a 'display phrase' that will allow you to put a font through its paces, check there's nothing untoward.

The quick brown fox jumps over the lazy dog is not a perfect pangram, because it repeats letters. The truly perfect pangram would contain all the letters of the alphabet in the right order, but the only thing that achieves that is the alphabet. There are phrases that use fewer characters, but

It actually happens: the quick brown fox does his thing on YouTube

they are not as catchy. And this is not for want of trying. Here are two of the shortest:

Quick wafting zephyrs vex bold Jim.
Sphinx of black quartz judge my vow.

And here are a couple that make a kind of sense:

Zany eskimo craves fixed job with quilting party.
Playing jazz vibe chords quickly excites my wife.

However, they are not serious rivals. Not the kind of thing that would inspire 300,000 or so people to watch the video on YouTube where the phrase comes to life. The video (and you *must* watch) features a fox, slightly more grey than brown, jumping over a dog. It needs a couple of attempts to make the clearance, and the dog just stands there, oblivious to its contribution to type history. But letter lovers who have seen this astounding feat have found the video world-changing. 'Wow, this actually happens in real life,' commented Jackewilton. And tmc515 summed it up for all time: 'Ladies and Gentlemen, I believe our work here is done.'

Type foundries like to ring the changes with their display phrases. Browse old specimen books, or modern online sites, and you will find a whole range of sayings, often evoking the font in question, sometimes by means of a pangram.

A few of them are composed by type designers and reference their trade. Jonathan Hoefler reckons you could *Mix Zapf with Veljovic and get quirky Beziers*. While Hermann Zapf asserted *Typography is known for two-dimensional architecture and requires extra zeal within every job*. Zapf's phrase also works in German: *Typographie ist zweidimensionale Architektur und bedingt extra Qualität in jeder vollkommenen Ausführung*. And there are other good pangrams in French (*Portez ce vieux whisky au juge blond qui fume*, which translates as 'Take this old whiskey to the blond judge who smokes'), and Dutch (*Zweedse ex-VIP, behoorlijk gek op quantumfysica*, which means 'Swedish ex-VIP, pretty crazy about quantum physics'.)

Type designers clearly find the pangram an important display tool, engaging the mind in a way that ABCDE does not. But what happens when a phrase becomes just too long?

Is there a shorter and more arresting way of performing a similar job?

When Paul Renner designed Futura, his display phrase was **Die schrift unserer Zeit** ('The font of our time'). But that was a statement of intent; clearly not every new typeface could make that claim. One that could was Univers, the classic Swiss type by Adrian Frutiger. When this appeared in a lavish book celebrating his work, it was displayed in a text written by Frutiger himself:

> You may ask why so many different typefaces. They all serve the same purpose but they express man's diversity. It is the same diversity we find in wine. I once saw a list of Medoc wines featuring 60 different Medocs all of the same year. All of them were wines but each were different from the others. It's the nuances that are important. The same is true of typefaces.

The Frutiger book is not, however, a marketing tool available to most new fonts, which at best have a narrow column in online catalogues to sell their wares. For decades one word has usually sufficed: *Hamburgers* or *Hamburgerfont*. This successfully showed off the characters of a new typeface that would most distinguish it from its competitors: the h, g and e have always expressed their own individuality.

When Matthew Carter starts work on a new font, he usually first draws an h, followed by an o and a p and a d. It sets the tone for letters that follow, and hopefully creates the correct sense of height, width and balance. But it is only when his letters are placed side by side – when they relate to each other – that he can see whether he's on to something or if it's time to start afresh.

A word like *Hamburgerfont* will usually tell you straight off, for it provides all the major curves and abutments in regular usage. And if you're in the process of choosing a new type to use from a long list, then it's handy to have the same word repeated to use as a comparison. The typeface foundry URW was based in Hamburg and may be the source of the word (it has also been *Hamburgevons* and *Hamburgefontsiv*). It has also been used in the catalogues of the other major type suppliers ITC, Monotype and Adobe. Agfa often used Championed. The Letraset catalogues favoured Lorem Ipsum Dolor.

Now there is a new(ish) word: *Handgloves*.

The digital type library FontShop sells many thousands of fonts designed all over the world. The names of the bestsellers will usually be followed by the letters OT, short for OpenType, which means the font is seamlessly usable on multiple operating systems. These are, unsurprisingly, mostly text faces you can actually use in approachable and professional ways (ie they aren't mad like FF Dirtyfax, which looks as if you have pulled a sheet of A4 through a paperjam). They have been produced by different designers who have licensed their work to a chosen foundry. As with most things digital, the old order has crumbled in its wake.

Eighty years ago, most countries had a handful of traditional foundries supplying a choice of typefaces to those who bought their typesetting and printing services.

AaBbCc Handgloves

Do Not Adjust Your Eyes: Dirtyfax

They would employ in-house designers, and their styles were necessarily conservative; there was no point in spending months on a fancy font that no one used. Occasionally something unpredictable broke through – Paul Renner making Futura for the Bauer Type Foundry in Frankfurt, Eric Gill making Gill Sans for Monotype in Surrey, Rudolf Koch making Kabel for the Klingspor Foundry in Offenbach – but it wasn't like today, where it is hard to distinguish the revolutionary from the bizarre.

Every couple of weeks, FontShop staff email their clients a list of new designs. Many are stylish and practical, others look like clever graphic stunts that would seem hard to use in any context. But still they fill up the inbox every fortnight, and even the most willing recipient will have a hard time keeping up. And so a new method of display has been devised. Rather than ten letters of each new typeface showing in *Handgloves* and the rest of the alphabet shown beneath it, each font now comes with words unique to its character, style and possible use.

The font Lombriz is displayed in the catalogue by the phrase *Daily Special* – it looks a little like the Kellogg's signature on cereal boxes.

The font Flieger is shown off best with the words *MustangTurbo*, as if in chrome on the trunk of a Cadillac.

The phrase employed to describe the typeface FF Chernobyl seems a little heartless: **Removes unwanted hair**.

'It's one of my favourite things to do,' Stephen Coles says at the FontShop office in San Francisco. 'You get to play with type, pick the characters that are most interesting, and do what you want with them. For a type lover it's like porn.'

Coles has the title of Type Director at FontShop and he will confess to the occasional collision with an object in the street as he looks up to admire a shop sign. His official biography says he is 'currently dating FF Tisa after breaking off a long and passionate affair with Motter Femina'. At the open-plan office in San Francisco, he produced some recent examples of new fonts, which he and his colleagues were selling with the words **VOLTAGE** (for the metallic and industrial PowerStation font), *Homage* (for the curly and delicate Anglia Script) and Bogart (for the lower-case very rounded Naiv).

'You concentrate on what glyphs in this typeface give it its distinctiveness,' he explained, 'and make sure that those are included in the sample. We try to think where the font would be used. If it's a newspaper's typeface we might do a headline. But if it's a fancy typeface we wouldn't just do an invitation to a wedding, we would try to be a little more sly about it. We also don't want to give a typeface a set use right away by limiting how it's displayed – you want it to feel versatile. And the display is very important. You can have a font that is really well designed, but if you don't display it well it's not going to sell. It's like taking a bad photograph of a sofa.' (Coles is also a fan of classic modernist furniture.)

I asked him about *Handgloves*. He said, 'It's got the straights in the h, it's got the a and the g, which are the most distinctive parts of any typeface, it shows the way a curve meets a straight in the n and the d, and it's got the round with the o and the diagonals with the v. It's got ascenders, descenders and it feels good as a shape.' Literally and figuratively, it contains a font's DNA. 'But we're trying to come up with a new standard word now. We're trying to drop *Handgloves*. We've had *Handgloves* for a while now.'

Coles introduced me to Chris Hamamoto, who had a long list of *Handgloves* alternatives on his computer. Anyone in the office could add to it, but there were certain guidelines:

The key letters, in order of importance, are: g, a, s, e. Then there is: l, o, I. And of lesser importance but still helpful: d (or b), h, m (or n), u, v.

Verbs or generic nouns are preferable because they don't describe the font (like adjectives) or confuse the sample word with a font name (like proper nouns).

Avoid tandem repeating letters unless showing off alternatives.

Use one word, as spaces can get too large and distracting at display sizes.

The words selected by FontShop staff were: *Girasole*, *Sage oil*, *Dialogues*, *Legislator*, *Coalescing*, *Anthologies*, *Genealogist*, *Legislation*, *Megalopolis*, *Megalopenis*, *Rollerskating* and *gasoline*. Then there was a secondary list, which used at least four of the key letters: *Majestic*, *Salinger*, *Designable*, *Harbingers*, *Webslinger*, *Skatefishing*, *Masquerading* and … *Handgloves*. And for some reason that nobody could quite define – possibly familiarity, possibly because of the same visual instinct that scaled its choice in the first place – *Handgloves* still looked the best.

On the day I visited, Hamamoto was working on an email display of some fresh type specimens. He said he drew inspiration from books, Internet searches and rap music. I had received his latest email the day before, which included **Regime**, a font by British designer Jonathan Barnbrook working at the Virus foundry, whose work was influenced by nineteenth-century slab-serif Empire fonts and was described by Hamamoto as political, and which he had illustrated with the phrases **first apparent heir**, **election** and **conservative progressive**.

There was also Aunt Mildred, which had a spidery feel and was shown with lines of gothic poetry, and *Henrietta Samuels*, from the flowery hand of a Swedish calligrapher, which had reminded the FontShop staff of old-fashioned candy wrappers: 'The capital E is really gorgeous!' Stephen Coles said. But the one recent font that the people at FontShop seemed most excited about was Rocky. As their blurb went, 'New typefaces by legendary designer Matthew Carter come few and far between, so Rocky naturally grabbed our attention.' The design had come about because Carter had been wondering why no Bodoni-style fonts (the face with the high contrast thick and thin strokes) had Latin serifs (which were almost triangular). Rocky was the answer, and came in forty different styles, including Rocky Light, **Rocky Black**, and Rocky Regular.

Rocky was displayed in the catalogue with the obscure hip-hop phrases **extra rep – show him how you feel** and Dough tops like a hot scoff. It looked exquisite, but the words appeared meaningless; clearly, the type was in control now.

The Worst Fonts In the World

We'd need another book, of course, to do this justice. And where would one start?

Fonts are like cars on the street – we notice only the most beautiful or ugly, the funniest or the flashiest. The vast majority roll on regardless. There may be many reasons why we dislike or distrust certain fonts, and overuse and misuse are only starting points. Fonts may trigger memory as pungently as perfume: **Gill Sans** can summon up exam papers. TRAJAN may remind us of lousy choices at the cinema (you'll see it on the posters of more bad films than any other font) and gruelling evenings with Russell Crowe. There was a time when it looked as though he would only appear in films – A BEAUTIFUL MIND, MASTER AND

COMMANDER, MYSTERY, ALASKA – if the marketing team promised to use Trajan in its pseudo-Roman glory on all its promotional material (There is a funny and rather alarming YouTube clip about this: search for 'Trajan is the Movie Font'.)

Most of the time we only notice typeface mistakes, or things before or behind their times. In the 1930s, people tutted over Futura and predicted fleeting fame; today we may be outraged by the grunge fonts BLACKSHIRT and AFTERSHOCK DEBRIS, but in a decade they may be everywhere, and a decade after that we may be bored with their blandness.

Fortunately, choosing the worst fonts in the world is not merely an exercise in taste and personal vindictiveness – there has been academic research. In 2007, Anthony Cahalan published his study of font popularity (or otherwise) as part of Mark Batty's *Typographic Papers Series (Volume 1)*. He had sent an online questionnaire to more than a hundred designers, and asked them to identify:

a) the fonts they used most,
b) the ones they believed were most highly visible,
c) the ones they liked least.

The Top Tens were:

Used Regularly:
1. Frutiger (23 respondents)
2. Helvetica/Helvetica Neue (21)
3. Futura (15)

4. **Gill Sans** (13)

5. Univers (11)

6. Garamond (10)

7= Bembo; Franklin Gothic (8)

9. Minion (7)

10. Arial (6)

Highly Visible:

1. Helvetica/Helvetica Neue (29)

2. **Meta** (13)

3. Gill Sans (9)

4. Rotis (8)

5. Arial (7)

6. ITC Officina Sans (4)

7. Futura (3)

8= ***Bold Italic Techno***; FF Info; Mrs Eaves; Swiss;
    TheSans; Times New Roman (2)

Least Favourite:

1. Times New Roman (19)

2. Helvetica/Helvetica Neue (18)

3. *Brush Script* (13)

4= Arial; Courier (8)

6= Rotis; Souvenir (6)

8. **Grunge Fonts** (generic) (5)

9= **Avant Garde**; Gill Sans (4)

11. Comic Sans (3)

The Least Favourite survey contained brief explanations.
Twenty-three respondents said the fonts were misused or

overused; 18 believed they were ugly; others found them to be boring, dated, impractical or clichéd; 13 expressed either dislike or blind hatred.

This was not the first such survey to be conducted. There seems to be a new one every year online, but they tend to concentrate, rightly, on best fonts. Occasionally a novel theory emerges, such as the opinion expressed by the designer Mark Simonson on the Typophile forum. Simonson believes that some typefaces are 'novice magnets', possessing properties that draw in those with an untrained eye but a desire to impress. 'To the average person, most fonts look more or less the same. But, if a typeface has a strong flavour, it calls attention to itself. It's easy to recognize and makes people feel like they know something about fonts when they recognize it. And it looks "special" compared to normal (ie boring) fonts, so using it makes their documents look "special". To the experienced designer, such typefaces have too much flavour, call too much attention to themselves, not to mention the fact that they often carry the baggage of being associated with amateur design.'

The choice of the Worst Typefaces in the World that follows may appear to be purely subjective, like the choice of most reviled pop singer or most hilarious fashion crime. And so it is. But there is also a broad consensus about what constitutes awfulness in type. As we have seen, the one thing that most people (type professionals and laypeople combined) agree on is that Comic Sans is no good at all. But it is harmless and even benign, and, on account of its unassuming beginnings, perhaps does not deserve the loathing that has been heaped upon it. But what can you say about the virtually illegible outer-limits fonts: *Grassy*, for example: a type with hair; or *Scrawlz*, which looks like writing by a 3- or 103-year-old?

These targets, though, are just too easy, and it would be like criticizing your child's acting in the nativity play. By contrast, the names in the list below, designed by professionals for reward and approval, have had it coming for a while. Here then, in reverse order, are my nominations for the eight worst fonts in the world.

8 Ecofont

One ought to approve. Ecofont is designed to save ink, money and eventually the planet, but heaven save us from worthy fonts. Ecofont is a program that adds holes to a font. The software takes Arial, Verdana, Times New Roman and prints them as if they had been attacked by moths. They retain their original shape, but not their inner form, and so lose their true weight and beauty. They also usually go no bigger than 11pt, although at this size or smaller they may save you 25 per cent of ink consumption.

The plus side: In 2010 Ecofont won a European Environmental Design Award. The down side: a study at the University of Wisconsin

Ecofont – giving Greens a bad press?

claimed that some Ecofont fonts, such as Ecofont Vera Sans, actually use more ink and toner than lighter regular fonts such as Century Gothic (although one could, of course, always print Century Gothic using Ecofont software).

The verdict: the string vest and Swiss Cheese of fonts; a nice idea for printing large documents in draft – but do you really need to print them at all?

7 Souvenir

'Real men don't set Souvenir,' wrote the type scholar Frank Romano in the early 1990s, by which time he had already been performing character assassination on the type for over a decade. At every opportunity in print and online, Romano would have a go. 'Souvenir is a font fatale ... We could send Souvenir to Mars, but there are international treaties on pollution in outer space ... remember, friends don't let friends set Souvenir.'

Souvenir bold – it peaked with 1970s soft porn

26
good
reasons
to use
Souvenir
Light

We'll get back to you ...

Romano is not alone; Souvenir seems to infuriate more type designers than practically anything else. Peter Guy, who has designed books for the Folio Society, wonders, 'Souvenir of what, I would like to know?' He has a possible answer: 'A souvenir of every ghastly mistake ever made in type design gathered together – with a few never thought of before – into one execrable mish-mash.' And even the people who sell it hate it. Here is Mark Batty from International Typeface Corporation (ITC) on one of his best-selling fonts: 'A terrible typeface. A sort of *Saturday Night Fever* typeface wearing tight white flared pants ...'

Souvenir was the Comic Sans of its era, which was the 1970s before punk. It was the face of friendly advertising, and it did indeed appear on Bee Gees albums, not to mention the pages of Farrah Fawcett-era *Playboy*. Oddly, though, Souvenir was far from a Seventies face. It was cut in 1914 by the American Type Founders Company, one of the many fonts of Morris Fuller Benton. After a bit of attention it died away, and that would have been that, had it not been revived by ITC half a century later and given a big push in the heyday of photocomposition.

Souvenir has been in the wilderness for two decades, hiding from a design community critical of anything once described as 'warm and fuzzy', but bizarrely it is almost hip again, at least in the pages of the design magazines. One may be rightfully suspicious of ironic retro patronage, but in this case there is genuine enthusiasm. 'Every character is a graphic icon, but as a typeface it is still harmonious,' believes Jason Smith, the founder of the Fontsmith foundry, who once chose the lowercase g of Souvenir Demi Bold as his favourite single character of all time ('the soft terminals and rounded organic body – gorgeous').

6 Gill Sans Light Shadowed

Gill Sans Light Shadowed is the sequel that should never have been made – a font that pleases the taxman and no one else. It's hard to believe that this is what Eric Gill had in mind when he first picked up chisel and quill – a type design that would combine the look of both but ultimately end up redolent only of crackly Letraset on a school magazine.

Gill Sans Light Shadowed – don't try this at home

Gill Sans Light Shadowed is an optical font defined by its black dimensional shadow, designed to suggest the effect the sun would cast over thin raised letters. Like an Escher drawing, it will soon induce headaches, the brain struggling to cope with the perfection and exactitude.

There are a great deal of similar three-dimensional effects on the market, the majority from the late 1920s and 1930s – Plastika, Semplicita, Umbra and Futura Only Shadow – and many digital shaded fonts such as Refracta and Eclipse suggest the trend has not worn itself out. Like the many fonts designed to resemble old-fashioned typewriters – Courier, American Typewriter, Toxica – the effect amuses for a very limited time, leaving cumbersome words that are difficult to read and lack all emotion.

5 *Brush Script*

If, during the 1940s, you were ever persuaded by government posters to *bathe with a friend* or *dig for victory*, the persuading was probably done in Brush Script. If, during the 1960s or 70s, you worked on a college or community magazine, then Brush Script screamed, *Use me. I look like handwriting.* If, during the 1990s, you ever perused the menu of a local restaurant (the sort of restaurant opened by people who on a starlit evening thought, 'I'm a pretty good cook – I think I'll open a restaurant!'), then that menu had a good chance of featuring *Pear, Blue Cheese and Walnut Salad on a Bed of Brush Script.* And if, in the twenty-first century, you ever even momentarily considered putting Brush Script on any document at all, even in an ironic way, then you should immediately relinquish all claims to taste.

Brush Script was made available by American Type Founders (ATF) in 1942, and its designer Robert E Smith gave it a lower case with joining loops, creating a quaint and consistent type that looked as if it was written by a fluid, carefree human. The problem was, no one you had ever met actually wrote like that, with such perfect weight distribution and no smudges (and of course every f, g and h exactly the same as the last one). But it seemed like a good type for corporations and government bodies to get what they wanted across in a non-corporate way, which is why advertisers used it so much for three decades. It was also the type that introduced Kylie Minogue, Jason Donovan and *Neighbours* to the world in 1985, a rare instance of opening

Brush Script – the case rests

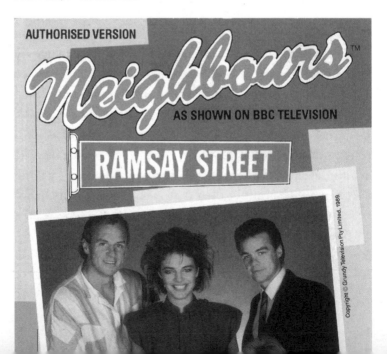

credits that looked as though they had been written by an elderly member of the cast.

Brush Script inspired a hundred more handwriterly alternatives – Mistral, Chalkduster, Avalon, Reporter, Riva. Many of these are rather nice, and some (Cafe Mimi, Calliope, and HT Gelateria) are lavishly beautiful. Every leading digital foundry offers an extensive list, ranging from childish scrawl to technical precision. But they all have one thing in common: they are trying to fool you into thinking they are not made on a computer, and they never succeed.

There are also a number of companies that offer you the chance to create a font from your own handwriting. With a site like fontifier.com this is almost instant: you fill in an alphabet grid, upload it (with your payment) for digital rendering, and you'll be able to preview your own uniquely named type with hundreds of professional script fonts, and perhaps discover that it's better than many.

4 Papyrus

Avatar cost more to make than any other film in history but it did its best to recoup whatever it spent on 3-D special effects and computer-generated blue people by using the cheapest and least original font it could find: Papyrus, a font available free on every Mac and PC. They did tweak it a little for the posters, but they used the standard version for credits and the subtitling for the Na'vi conversations. And it seems to have been a very conscious move from the top. On the website iheartpapyrus.com you'll see James Cameron briefing star Sam Worthington in a T-shirt proudly asserting 'Papyrus 4 Ever!'

Cameron's choice was baffling. Papyrus is not a bad font on its own, but is so clichéd and overused that its prominent selection for a genre-busting movie seems perverse. It also seems geographically inappropriate: as everyone who has written a school project over the last decade will tell you, Papyrus is the font you use to spell out the word Egypt.

Papyrus – something of a cult

Designed by Chris Costello and released by Letraset in 1983, Papyrus suggests what it might be like to use a quill on Egyptian plant-like material. The letters have notches and roughness, and give a good account of a chalk or crayon fraying at the edges. The primitive letters leave the impression of writing in a hurry but there is also a consistency to the style, with E and F both carrying unusually high cross-bars. The lower case seemed to be modelled closely on the early twentieth-century American newspaper favourite Cheltenham.

The font soon became a favourite of Mediterranean-style restaurants, amusing greeting cards, and amateur productions of Joseph and his Amazing Technicolour Dreamcoat (long title – good in Papyrus Condensed), and its digital incarnation proved perfect for the desktop publishing boom of the mid-1980s.

It said adventurous and exotic, and marked its user out as a would-be Indiana Jones. Its use in *Avatar* was a remarkable notch up – and another example of growing typographic literacy as moviegoers scratched their heads and wondered where they had seen those titles before.

#3 NEULAND INLINE

Are you out this evening to see an amateur stage version of a musical involving an animal called Pumbaa and another called Timon, with songs performed by a junior Elton John? Good luck! While you're there, take a look at the poster. More likely than not it will be in **NEULAND** or **NEULAND INLINE**. The Neuland family says Africa in the same way as Papyrus says Egypt, albeit the it's-all-good safari/ spear-dance side of Africa rather than the shanty-town or Aids side. It is a dense and angular type, suggestive of something Fred Flintstone might chisel into prehistoric rock. The inline version is bristling with energy and a quirkiness of spirit, a bad type predominantly through its overuse rather than its construction.

Neuland Inline – a font with a health warning

Neuland was created in 1923 by the influential typographer Rudolf Koch, who also made Kabel, Marathon and Neufraktur. At the time of release it was so far removed from other German types (both blackletter and the emerging modernists) that it was widely regarded with derision – too clumsy and inflexible. But its individuality soon became its strength, and by 1930 it had been adopted to advertise products that thought of themselves as special: the **RUDGE-WHITWORTH** four-speed motorcycle; **ENO'S FRUIT SALTS**; **AMERICAN SPIRIT** cigarettes. Some time later, as with Papyrus, Neuland hit the big time in the movies – with the type almost as prominent in **JURASSIC PARK** as the dinosaurs.

Both Neuland and Papyrus are classifiable as theme park fonts, more comfortable on the big rides at Universal Studios, Busch Gardens or Alton Towers than they are on the page. There are many other display types that share this dubious attribute, and the enterprising man behind a site called MickeyAvenue.com has spent a great deal of time at Walt Disney World Resort in Florida noting them all down. We now know to expect Kismet at the Corner Café on Main Street, and **JUNIPER** at the Haunted Mansion, while ᴜɪʙʀᴀ, which was put on this earth to spell the word ᴊoustɪɴɢ, is at Magic Kingdom's Fantasyland. The classics, too, show up in places their designers could never have envisaged. Albertus reigns at the Animal Kingdom Oasis area; Gill Sans provides signage at the Epcot Imagination zone; Univers does its usual information duty at transportation and ticketing areas, while Futura is at the Animal Kingdom's Dino Institute.

You may write to the MickeyAvenue webmaster thanking him for his sterling endeavours. You will receive a reply thanking you for your communication written – of course – in Papyrus.

#2 Ransom Note

As you might expect, Ransom Note consists of letters that look as if they have been hurriedly cut from magazines to form unnerving messages. There are various styles of such fonts available, many of them downloadable free of charge, and you might use them to write such things as Pay up

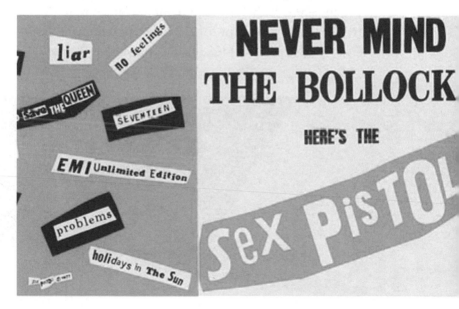

The Sex Pistols demonstrate correct use of ransom note type in the days before digital fonts made it a bit too easy

or the kitten gets it. Inevitably these menaces don't look very realistic, and Ransom Note is a font best used for comic effect, perhaps to say Christian is having another bloody paintballing birthday party – please do come.

The names are often better than the type – BlackMail, Entebbe, Bighouse. None of them, however, have a genuine ransom note's sweat, glue and menace, nor the cut-up shock-art of those original Sex Pistols record sleeves.

#1 The 2012 Olympic Font

Precisely 800 days before the Olympic Games were due to start, the Official London 2012 shop began selling miniature die-cast taxis in pink, blue, orange and other shades, the

2012 Headline: will we learn to love this font?

first of forty such models, each promoting a different sport. The cabs are not like the lovingly crafted ones you can buy from Corgi, with opening doors and jewelled headlights, more the lumpy ones sold in Leicester Square to tourists in a hurry.

Why should this matter? Because they are an example of very bad design, something London has largely begun to shun in recent years. What makes them doubly bad is the packaging, which comes with a bit of trivia about all the Olympic and Paralympic sports, each heralded with the question 'Did You Know?' in what is surely the worst new public typeface of the last 100 years.

The London 2012 Olympic Typeface, which is called 2012 Headline, may be even worse than the London 2012 Olympic Logo, but by the time it was released people were so tired of being outraged by the logo that the type almost passed by unnoticed. The Logo was the subject of immediate parody (some detected Lisa Simpson having sex, others a swastika), and even the subject of a health warning – an animated pulsing version was said to have brought on epileptic fits. In the *International Herald Tribune*, Alice Rawsthorn observed that 'it looks increasingly like the graphic equivalent of what we Brits scathingly call "dad dancing" – namely a middle-aged man who tries so hard to be cool on the dance floor that he fails'.

Like the logo, the uncool font is based on jaggedness and crudeness, not usually considered attributes where sport is concerned. Or maybe it's an attempt to appear hip and down with the kids – it looks a little like the sort of tagging one might see in 1980s graffiti. It also has a vaguely Greek appearance, or at least the UK interpretation of Greek, the sort of lettering you will find at London kebab shops and restaurants called Dionysus. The slant to the letters is suddenly interrupted by a very round and upright o, which may be trying to be an Olympic Ring. The font does have a few things going for it: it is instantly identifiable, it is not easily forgettable, and because we'll be seeing so much of it, it may eventually cease to offend. Let's hope they keep it off the medals.

Just My Type

22

In September 2001, the printer manufacturer Lexmark asked its users a personal question: were they 'Nerd, Sex Kitten or Professional?' It was a promotional exercise designed to get the company's name in the papers, which it did, and it had the effect of giving computer users pause before they created their next CV or love letter. According to Lexmark, our choice of font sends a strong signal to others of our taste, and possibly our character.

A few months before, Lexmark had commissioned a man they called 'a Manhattan psychologist' to examine the psychology of fonts. This was Aric Sigman, a fellow of the Society of Biology, associate fellow of the British Psychological Society and fellow of the Royal Society of

Medicine. He was often in the news for his views on the effect of television and the Internet on child development. Sigman wasn't a font expert, but he had talked to about twenty people involved with font creation and sales, most of whom had already developed psychological font theories of their own. 'It wasn't deep science,' he told me years later, 'it was market research'. It was a study of something he calls social coding, an analysis of emotional connotations gleaned not by the users of certain fonts, but by those to whom they send their writing. Our choice of hairstyle, music or car may inadvertently display similar codes.

Sigman's findings were presented by Lexmark in a style that allowed no room for doubt.

Don't use Courier unless you want to look like a nerd. It's a favourite for librarians and data entry companies.

Alternatively, if you see yourself as a sex kitten, go for a soft and curvy font like Shelley.

People who use Sans Serif fonts like Univers tend to value their safety and anonymity.

Comic Sans, conversely, is the font for self-confessed attention-seekers because it allows for more expression of character.

As if these compelling generalizations weren't enough, there was also a quick survey of fonts of the rich and famous.

Jennifer Lopez and Kylie Minogue both apparently favoured *Shelley*. Richard Branson used Verdana. Ricky Martin (this was 2001) went for Palatino. And there was further advice on layout: 'If you're writing those life-altering letters make sure that the font is small and minimalist. Less is definitely more. Large fonts reveal certain insecurities.'

Interestingly, the people who worked in the Lexmark marketing department printed their report in Arial, displaying a desire for anonymity, and perhaps also a possible adherence to strict corporate policy.

Dr Sigman's full report contained a little more detail. 'Fonts with big round Os and tails are perceived as more human-like and friendly, perhaps because aspects of the font appear to mimic the human face. Fonts which are more rectilinear and angular conjure up overtones of rigidity, technology, coldness ... in psychoanalytic terms, [they are] emotionally repressed or anally retentive.'

He then went on to offer advice for particular situations. For a thank-you letter, Sigman suggested, one should use something straight and sincere with a buoyant air, perhaps Geneva. For a resignation letter – that depends if you enjoyed your employment (in which case an appealing font with a human edge, such as New York or Verdana), but if your time in the job was hell, then it's dispassionate Arial.

The best font for a love letter? Ideally something affectionate with big round Os, but you might also consider an italicized font such as *Humana Serif Light* which alludes to old-fashioned scribes and may possess '*a softening emotional quality, as if the writer is leaning over to talk personally to the reader*'.

But beware: '*Implementing such fonts may also serve as an aid to romantic deception*'.

And what, finally, should one use to end a relationship? 'For clarity without harshness,' the doctor prescribes plain old Times Regular. 'To let them down softly, italicized fonts can be employed. However, the user may unwittingly give the reader false hope. Verdana or Hoefler Text may have a lighter, optimistic yet respectful feel to it. For those who won't take no for an answer, Courier or the more rigid technical fonts indicate there's no room for misinterpretation, no going back.'

But why trust the survey of a popular psychologist? Why not conduct a survey of your own? At the end of 2009, the design company Pentagram sent out an elaborate e-card, as their season's greetings. Previously these had taken the form of booklets but this one was a link to an online questionnaire called **'What type are you?'** (the question posed in bold Helvetica Neue).

The survey (it is still online should you wish to take part) starts with a film-loop of your own personal font analyst in a consulting room – white painted wood panelling, Eileen Gray glass table. He is filmed from the neck down, so one notices the pad on his knee, his cufflinks and his corduroy trousers. 'What type are you?' the man asks in an Austrian or possibly Swiss accent (basically he's Freud). 'Answer four simple questions that will help you drink from the font of self-knowledge, face the truth and find out just which type you are. Fill in the required information.' This consists merely of your name, but the analyst is impatient. 'Quickly now,' he says as he swivels on his squeaky chair; a tinkling piano and a ticking clock add to the mood.

Once you have filled in your name, the four questions are: 'Are you Emotional – someone who's happy to say that something feels right? Or are you Rational – someone who prefers to say that something has a one-in-two chance of being right? Pick one please.' The analyst plays with his pen.

I click *Emotional*. The analyst writes down the answer on his pad. 'You are emotional – good. Second question: 'Are you Understated – someone who thinks the best word is a word in your ear? Or are your Assertive – someone who believes that the word in your ear is best shouted? Make your mind up please.'

I click *Understated*. He writes it down. 'Let's move on. Third question: are you Traditional – someone who believes

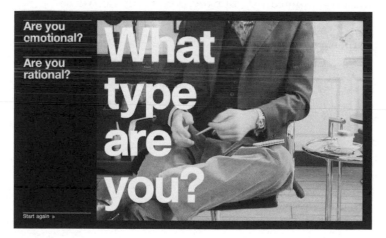

What type are you? The analyst awaits your answers ...

that ideas, like wine, are best aged? Or are you Progressive
– someone who believes that ideas, like milk, are best fresh?
Quickly now.' The analyst stirs his coffee as, naturally, I opt
for *Progressive*.

'You are progressive. To the last question now. Are you
Relaxed? Are you someone who takes any chocolate from
the box and eats it whether hazelnut crunch or orange
cream? Or are you Disciplined – someone who suffers the
orange cream first so they can save the hazelnut crunch till
last? Come on, come on.' A fly buzzes around him as I pick
Disciplined.

Before the analyst recaps my choices and finds my type, I
remember a comment from Eric Gill from the middle of the
last century: 'There are now about as many different varieties
of letters as there are different kinds of fools.' So what kind
of fool am I? My analyst could have chosen Cooper Black
Italic, Bifur, Corbusier Stencil or one of sixteen others on
the programmed list. But my type turns out to be Archer
Hairline, and photographs of this handsome font appear
with a spoken explanation:

Designed by Jonathan Hoefler and Tobias Frere-
Jones, Archer Hairline is a modern typeface with a
straightforward appearance, but one that has tiny
outbreaks of elegance and tiny dots of emotion, only
apparent on closer examination. If you are someone who
is outwardly composed, but will occasionally run into the
bathroom for a quick laugh or quiet cry before emerging
to the world outwardly composed again, then Archer
Hairline is your type.

Expanded Antique, font of choice for a select group

How popular is my type? When I subjected it to online analysis, some 278,000 people had been before me and the most common results had been Dot Matrix (13.3 per cent), Archer Hairline (11.4), universal (9.9), Courier (9.7) and **Cooper Black Italic** (9.5). Down at the bottom, only 1.6 per cent were deemed to be **Expanded Antique**.

Surveys such as this can cause low self-esteem; too bad if you always thought of yourself as Georgia and Font Freud says you're **Souvenir**.

Things have changed beyond measure since Steve Jobs put a little font choice on his Apple computers. The most basic Mac now comes with twenty-three variants of Lucida and eleven of Gill Sans, as well as ones that seldom see the light of day, such as Haettenschweiler and Harrington. And Windows users aren't short of a face these days, either, with Arab, Thai and Tamil scripts bundled into Windows 7 along with dozens of regular fonts.

And if none of these feel quite right to you, there is always the option of making your own. Given the patience and the desire to create an A and a G that hasn't been made before, you can fire up one of a number of software programs – TypeTool, FontLab Studio and Fontographer are the most popular – and begin your quest.

If you click on 'New Font' in the Fontographer program, you get a grid for every conceivable letter and character, along with every accent in almost every language. You might click on 'a', and the grid opens up to a larger square. There are side-panels packed with tools to help you measure, triangulate, blend, retract, merge, hilite and hint. But basically your task is the same as it has been for centuries: you must make something beautiful and readable.

I asked Matthew Carter whether computers have made the life of a type designer any easier (Carter, you'll recall, began life as a punchcutter in the style of a latterday Gutenberg, and has worked with practically every typesetting method since; his greatest digital hits have been Verdana and Georgia). He replied, 'Some aspects get easier. But if you're doing a good job you should feel that it gets harder. If you think it's getting easier, you ought to look out. I think it means you're getting lazy.'

When personal computers and typographic software were in their infancy, Carter became involved in a quarrel at a type conference with the designer Milton Glaser (the

Milton Glaser's Baby Teeth

veteran designer who made the I ❤ New York logo and the hand-drawn typefaces Baby Teeth and Glaser Stencil). 'He was very resistant,' Carter remembers. 'His point was that you can't sketch with a computer, you can't do a woolly line – everything that comes out of a computer is finished. I didn't disagree with that, but on a computer there are other ways of sketching. All type design programs have these very crude tools that allow you to take a shape and flip and flop it and stick it here and there. And if I'm designing a typeface and I've drawn the lower-case b, there's information there that I can use for the p and the q, so why not flip and flop it? It's done in seconds, and it gives me a chance to clean things up and resolve matters. And if I've done a lower-case n, I've got a lot of information about the m and the h and the u. Why wouldn't I use that? In the old days when I was drawing it, I would also use that information but it would be much more laborious. Computers are not the answer, but they're a help.'

What then is the answer? After 560 years of movable type, why is our job not yet done? Why is the world still full of serious people trying to find great names for different new alphabets? The answer lies in another question. In 1968 the influential graphic design review *The Penrose Annual* asked exactly the same things: 'Aren't we done yet? Why do we need all these new fonts such as ... Helvetica?'

The answer, then and now, is the same. Because the world and its contents are continually changing. We need to express ourselves in new ways.

'I've got a whole talk called *Why New Typefaces?*' Matthew Carter adds. 'It's the most frequently asked question I get. There are only thirty-two notes on a tenor saxophone, and surely to God they've all been played by now. It's a bit like that with type – we are slicing the pie thinner and thinner. But at the same time, there are more good type designers now on the planet than at any other time in history.'

New technologies are making us familiar with new fonts and fonts previously obscure. The BlackBerry has BlackBerry Alpha Serif, Clarity and Millbank. The Amazon Kindle uses Monotype Caecillia. The iPad handles the same fonts as other Apple devices, and while its iBooks application carries a restrictive choice of fonts, there is a lavish app called *TypeDrawing*, which takes even the plainest fonts to exciting new heights; it may be the tool that teaches children about type – the modern version of the John Bull printing kit. You type in a phrase, or perhaps your name, and use your

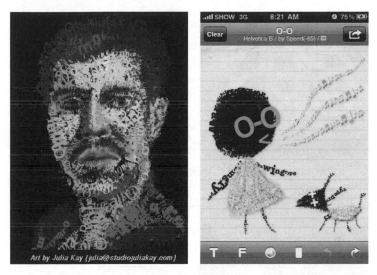

Art by Julia Kay {julia@studiojuliakay.com}

TypeDrawing fun on your shiny new Apple device

finger to paint a swirling picture with those word patterns on the screen. You can choose your colour, size and font – from Academy Engraved LET to *Zapfino* – and the results provide a whole new flowing definition of movable type.

Online you can also play *Cheese or Font*, a childish, fruitless and frustrating game in which a name appears on screen and you have to guess whether it's a ... yes, quite. Castellano? Molbo? Crillee? Arvore? Taleggio? You might do well to prepare for this by purchasing a set of Type Trumps – the designer's version of the kids' card game, with each font card rated for legibility, weight and special power.

After this it may come as a relief to waste at least five minutes of your time in the online company of 'Max Kerning'. Kerning is obsessed with kerning, the eradication of sloppy text by the correct proportional spacing. He

AVANT GARDE 2

CONTENTS

Year.................................1978
Price...........................£236
Cuts................................04
Rank...............................02
Legibility.........................06
Weights............................10
Foundry ....ITC
Designer................Herb Lubalin
Typeface................Avant Garde
Power.....Avant Garde Magazine

FRANKFURTER

PRICE
£105

YEAR
1970

CUTS
02

RANK
17

WEIGHTS
04

LEGIBILITY
04

DESIGNER
ALAN MEEKS

FOUNDRY
ADOBE

SPECIAL POWER
DUNKIN' DONUTS

---

foundry   typeface
the foundry   new alphabet

designer   weights
wim crouwel   03

year   price
1974   £113

rank   cuts
77   01

legibility   power
01   wim crouwel

Typeface_____Futura
Designer _____Paul Renner
Foundry _____Adobe
Year_____1927–1928
Price_____£278
Weights _____20
Rank _____04
Cuts_____05
Legibility_____06
Special Power ___ Stanley Kubrick

Know your fonts with Type Trumps

speaks with a hybrid Dutch and German accent, wears a tie beneath a gold-coloured jumper, and seems to have plastic hair. The video shows him vacuuming, and removing lint from his sleeve with a roller. 'Clean type is godly type,' he says. 'I care about text. Some people say that I care too much. They say to me, they say, "Max, you are too strict!" That is what sloppy people say. When text is clean, well-spaced and organized, it is then, and only then that I find perfection.'

In a small office in San Francisco's Market Street, one great new hope of type design is pushing a new array of letters around a computer screen in search of the future – or at least something that will pay the office bills. He is Rodrigo Xavier Cavazos (or RXC), principal of PSY/OPS Type Foundry, a place responsible for fonts such as PUEBLO, RETABLO and MARTINI @ JOE'S – each exploring new and inspiring boundaries of what type is capable of.

Cavazos is fond of saying that when he is not working on a font, he can be found working on another font. He has designed his office to resemble an ambient chill-out space in a club, lots of lava lamps and soft furnishings, and many of his types reflect this dreamy, slightly hallucinogenic mood. Every chair has a little sloping desk close by, like a miniature architectural drawing board. When we met in mid-morning, these chairs and desks were empty, but as the day progressed PSY/OPS staff arrived one by one, and with hardly any noise placed their Macs on the tables and began working, defining the type of tomorrow.

Cavazos himself is in his mid-forties. He started PSY/OPS in the mid-1990s, its name inspired by the pseudoscientific term for clandestine military propaganda and mind-manipulation. 'Type is a powerful behaviour modification tool,' he explains. 'Transparent to the consumer; transcendent to the designer who knows how to use it.' His most famous client is Electronic Arts (EA), the computer games company, for whom he made a sans-serif for use in many of their sports games. It is an industrial, slightly collegiate font, but much of his foundry's output is better suited to layouts for avant garde magazines and tattoo catalogues.

Cavazos's fascination with type began as a child when he received a 'magical' toy printing press. He tries to communicate this naive sense of excitement when he teaches type design at the California College of the Arts, instructing his students to start by doodling letters on a napkin. Unfortunately, it's all downhill from there. 'A lot of genius in a doodle is in the fuzz,' he regrets. 'As soon as you have to define something and make it cleaner, say the thickness of a point, then things start to dry up. Then it becomes a matter of balancing the inspiration – keeping in the spirit of the design, while having a workable, lovely treatment with good constructions.'

But how do you teach someone to make a great new font? Partly by looking at the past – at the Garamonds, the Caslons and the Baskervilles. The walls of the PSY/OPS office are covered with traditional letterpress posters, another art Cavazos tries to instill in his students. 'It's essential to have some visual knowledge of what's gone before, the classic types,' he says. 'You look at a classic design and there's a reason it's still strong centuries later. But on the other hand,

ABCDEFGHIJKL

PQRSTUVWXYZ

ÎÕØÜABCDEFGHIJK

ǪPQRSTUVWXYZÀÅÉ

The devil is in the detail: Retablo, designed by RXC

those designs have already been created, and you want to make something new. There has to be a structure and a heart that underlies it, and then you combine that with naive accidents, and it creates a liveliness and a special quality. You need to observe, look and draw. You need to get a muscle-sense.'

On another continent, other forms are taking shape. In a garden in Berlin, the Dutch type designer Luc(as) de Groot tells me why he began to spell his name with parentheses. It is a few days after his forty-sixth birthday, and there is still a little cake left, decorated with his name in dry capital sans serif letter biscuits from Russia. I eat a piece of parenthesis and an a.

De Groot is one of the leading lights of contemporary type design, someone who is setting the tone of how our words may look in ten or fifteen years' time. His interest began young: his father grew and sold tulips, and he remembers he used Letraset Baskerville Italic on special offers for his bulbs. He was also fascinated by his dad's Golfball typewriter – by the way you could change the way words looked on a page. He made his own first 'crappy' font at the age of six.

For the most part, De Groot makes fonts we find very useful. In his youth he had a vision for a typeface, perhaps made of symbols, that could be used universally throughout the world to reflect peaceable and warm communication, and he still nurtures such ideals. 'I like to think my type has a friendly atmosphere,' he says. 'Humanistic with soft curves, something that helps people communicate in a friendly way.'

De Groot has several claims to fame. He made the Thesis family of typefaces, an entire 'typographic system' combining TheSans, TheSerif and TheMix fonts in a vast and cohesive array of weights and possible uses. (He says he has seen this font family on condoms, toilet paper, soap packaging, a bank in Poland and much of the east German

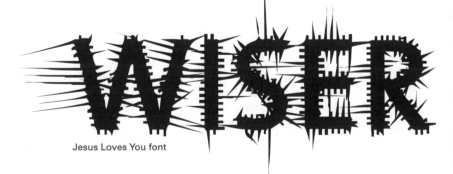

Jesus Loves You font

Luc(as) de Groot, designer of the world's most widely-used font – and it's not the Helvetica letters on the wall behind him...

city of Chemnitz.) He has redesigned logos for VW and Audi, and the masthead for *Der Spiegel*. And he has also made fonts that tread the outer limits: the crazy and aggressive font Jesus Loves You, for example, all thorns and barbed wire, or the soft floating Nebulae, made up of bubbles.

It was in 2002, however, that De Groot began his most significant work – a design that was to become another step-change in the history of type. He remembers a phone call with 'a go-between who asked me to design a font for a very secret client. I found out afterwards that it was Microsoft. It was a great feeling – I immediately started knocking down walls and redoing the office. But it was

a one-off payment, and if I had known it would have
been used the way it was I probably would have asked for
more money.'

Microsoft had called De Groot because it was looking
for new fonts for its ClearType initiative, a new technology
that offered increased clarity on a screen, and which was
developed initially for ebooks. De Groot offered them
Consolas, a highly stylized font that offered the apparent
simplicity of a typewriter style such as Courier with a depth
and warmth not normally associated with such a utilitarian
face. This swiftly became an integral part of the company's
Vista operating system.

But it was the type that De Groot designed next, Calibri,
that made most impact. In fact, it's fair to say that it has
changed the whole look of mass communication. Calibri is
a rounded, pliable sans serif with great visual impact, and

Calibri The quick brown fox jumps over the lazy dog abcdefgABCDEFG

Calibri rules the western world – for now

in 2007 it became Microsoft's font of choice, the default not only for Word (where it replaced the serif Times New Roman), but also for Outlook, PowerPoint and Excel (where it replaced Arial).

This made it the most widely used font in the western world. But did it also make it the best font? Or the most versatile? Or the most seductive, surprising and beautiful? Of course not. That font is yet to come.

Bibliography

Baines, Phil and Dixon, Catherine
Signs: Lettering in the Environment
Laurence King Publishing,
London, 2003

Baines, Phil and Haslam, Andrew
Type & Typography
Laurence King Publishing,
London, 2002

Ball, Johnson
William Caslon: Master of Letters
Kineton: The Roundwood Press,
Warwick, 1973

Banham, Mary & Hillier, Bevis (eds)
*A Tonic to the Nation: The Festival
of Britain 1951*
Thames and Hudson, London, 1976

Bartram, Alan
Typeforms: A History
The British Library & Oak Knoll
Press, London, 2007

Biggs, John R.
An Approach to Type
Blandford Press, London, 1961

Burke, Christopher
Paul Renner: The Art of Typography
Hyphen Press, London, 1988

Calahan, Anthony
*Type, Trends and Fashion (The
Typographic Papers Series)*
Mark Batty Publisher Academic,
New York City, 2007

Carter, Harry
*A View of Early Typography
Up to About 1600*
Hyphen Press, London, 2002

Cheng, Karen
Designing Type
Laurence King Publishing,
London, 2006

Child, Heather (ed)
*Edward Johnson:
Formal Penmanship*
Lund Humphries, London, 1971

Cramsie, Patrick
The Story of Graphic Design
British Library Publishing,
London, 2010

Dowding, Geoffrey
*An Introduction to the History of
Printing Types*
Wace & Company, London, 1961

Fenton, Erfert
*The Macintosh Font Book
2nd Edition*
Peachpit Press, California, 1991

Friedl, Friedrich; Ott, Nicolaus;
Stein, Bernard
*Typography: An Encyclopaedic
Survey of Type Design and
Techniques Throughout History*
Black Dog & Leventhal Publishers
Inc, New York, 1998

Frutiger, Adrian
Typefaces – the Complete Works.
Birkhauser, Basel, Boston, Berlin,
2009

Gill, Eric
An Essay on Typography,
London, 1936

Goudy, Frederic W.
Typologia
Berkeley, 1977

Gray, Nicolete
*Nineteenth-Century
Ornamented Typefaces*
Faber, 1976

Heller, Steven and Meggs, Philip B.
*Texts on Type: Critical Writings
on Typography*
Allworth Press, New York, 2001

Howes, Justin
Johnston's Underground Press
Capital Transport Publishing,
London, 2000

Johnson, Edward
Writing, Illuminating & Lettering
Sir Isaac Pitman & Sons,
London, 1945

Judson, Muriel
Lettering For Schools
Dryad Handicrafts
London, *c.* 1927

Kinneir, Jock
Words & Buildings
The Architectural Press,
London, 1980

Lawson, Alexander
Anatomy of a Typeface
Godine, Boston, 1990

Letterform Collected
*A Typographic Compendium
2005–09*
Grafik Magazine, London, 2009

Lowry, Martin
The World of Aldus Manutius
Basil Blackwell, Oxford, 1979

Loxley, Simon
Type: The Secret History of Letters
IB Tauris, London, 2004

MacCarthy, Fiona
Eric Gill
Faber and Faber, London 1989

Macmillan, Neil
An A-Z of Type Designers
Laurence King Publishing,
London, 2006

McLean, Ruari (ed)
Typographers on Type
Lund Humphries, London, 1995

McLuhan, Marshall
The Gutenberg Galaxy
University of Toronto Press, 1962

McMurtrie, Douglas C.
Type Design
John Lane The Bodley Head,
London, 1927

Middendorp, Jan and
Spiekermann, Erik
Made With FontFont
BIS Publishers, Amsterdam, 2006

Millman, Debbie
*Essential Principles of
Graphic Design*
RotoVision, Switzerland, 2008

Norton, Robert (ed)
*Types Best Remembered/
Types Best Forgotten*
Parsimony Press, Kirkland,
Washington, 1993

Pardoe, F.E.
*John Baskerville of Birmingham,
Letter-Founder and Printer*
Frederick Muller Ltd, London, 1975

*Penrose Annual 1957, 1962, 1967,
1968, 1969, 1976, 1980*
Lund Humphries, London

Perfect, Christopher
The Complete Typographer
Little, Brown and Company,
London, 1992

Perfect, Christopher and
Rookledge, Gordon
*Rookledge's Classic International
Typefinder*
Laurence King Publishing,
London, 2004

Rothenstein, Julian and
Gooding, Mel
*ABZ: More Alphabets and
Other Signs*
Redstone Press, London, 2003

Spiekermann, Erik and Ginger, E.M.
*Stop Stealing Sheep & Find Out
How Type Works*
Adobe Press, California, 1993

Tidcombe, Marianne
The Doves Press
The British Library & Oak Knoll
Press, London, 2002

Truong, Mai-Linh Thi, Siebert,
Jurgen and Spiekermann, Erik
FontBook
FSI, Berlin, 2006

Unger, Gerard
While You're Reading
Mark Batty, New York, 2007

Updike, Daniel Berkeley
In the Day's Work
Harvard University Press,
Massachusetts, 1924

White, Alex W.
Thinking in Type
Allworth Press, New York, 2005

Willen, Bruce and Strals, Nolen
Lettering & Type
Princeton Architectural Press,
New York, 2009

Wolpe, Berthold
A Retrospective Survey
Merrion Press, London, 2005

Zapf, Hermann
*Hermann Zapf and His Design
Philosophy (Selected Articles)*
Society of Typographic Arts,
Chicago, 1987

Online

A personal selection of videos, blogs, typeface libraries and discussion sites.

Font foundries and retailers:

Adobe
www.adobe.com/type

Font Bureau
www.fontbureau.com

FontFeed
www.fontfeed.com

Font Haus
www.fonthaus.com

Fonts.com (Monotype Imaging)
www.fonts.com

FontShop
www.fontshop.com

Fontsmith
www.fontsmith.com

FSI FontShop International
www.fontfont.com

Google Font Directory
www.code.google.com/webfonts

ITC (International Typeface
Corporation)
www.itcfonts.com

Linotype
www.linotype.com

MyFonts
www.myfonts.com

Featured Designers:

Jonathan Barnbrook
www.barnbrook.net

Rodrigo Xavier Cavazos and
PSY/OPS
www.psyops.com

Vincent Connare
www.connare.com/

Emigre
www.emigre.com

Hoefler & Frere-Jones
http://typography.com

Luc(as) de Groot
www.lucasfonts.com

Jim Parkinson
www.typedesign.com/index.html

David Pearson
www.davidpearsondesign.com

Mark Simonson
www.ms-studio.com

Erik Spiekermann
www.edenspiekermann.com/en

General:

Cheese or Font
www.cheeseorfont.mogrify.org/play

Eye (International Review of
Graphic Design)
www.eyemagazine.com

Grafik (The Magazine for
Graphic Design)
www.grafikmag.com

Identifont
www.identifont.com

I Love Typography
www.ilovetypography.com

Pentagram: What Type Are You
www.pentagram.com/what-type-
are-you

St Bride Library
www.stbridefoundation.org

The Type Directors Club
www.tdc.org

The Type Museum
www.typemuseum.org

TypArchive
www.typarchive.com

Typographica
www.typograhica.org

Typophile
www.typophile.com

The Wynkyn de Worde Society
www.wynkyndeworde.co.uk

YouTube Favourites:

Helvetica vs Arial Fontfight
www.youtube.com/
watch?v=m6djQHeqMwQ

Font Conference on Zapf Dingbats
www.youtube.com/watch?v=i3k5oY
9AHHM&feature=channel

Michael Bierut on Helvetica:
www.youtube.com/
watch?v=VDLPAE9wLEU

Mrs Eaves – Write Here,
Right Now:
www.youtube.com/
watch?v=Nz3lXu3VxVg&
feature=fvw

The Quick Brown Fox …
www.youtube.com/watch?v=00E_
LVo_aTo

Trajan is the Movie Font:
www.youtube.com/
watch?v=t87QKdOJNv8

Acknowledgements

Fonts entered my life when I was five or six. I can hear my dad telling a man in a peaked cap to fill her up, and I can see huge illuminated signs proclaiming Shell, Esso and BP. Long before these images assumed negative connotations they were treats for the eye – a burst of colour in a dusky landscape, brilliant branding, letters that seemed to fall from the sky and promise relief, further adventures and sweets. I don't think I was aware of the differences in type until then. My interest remained fleeting, or at least submerged. I devoured comics, but I wasn't aware until recently that the *Beano* nameplate was always all-caps while the *Dandy* usually wasn't.

Everything changed in 1971, when I was eleven. My brother bought the T.Rex album *Electric Warrior* and then David Bowie's *Hunky Dory*, and type became paired to emotion. One spent a lot of time staring at record sleeves in those days, and I began my

visual literacy that way – the way the gold outline capitals (T.REX) mirrored the halo around Marc Bolan and his amp; how the swell of the Bowie type (Zipper, I now know) promises an expanding consciousness even before the needle hits the groove.

My type education has been expanding ever since, and has recently been boosted beyond measure by the vast knowledge and experience of those who have helped me with this book. My first and largest debt is to Mark Ellingham, my editor at Profile Books, who not only got me on board, but has also proved an untiring source of encouragement and erudition through every stage of writing and production. Everyone at Profile Books has been unswervingly supportive of this project from the beginning, and I particularly wish to thank Andrew Franklin, Stephen Brough, Niamh Murray, Penny Daniel, Pete Dyer, Rebecca Gray, Anna-Marie Fitzgerald, Diana Broccardo, Emily Orford, Michael Bhaskar and Daniel Crewe; proofreaders Penny Gardiner and Caroline Pretty, and indexer Diana Lecore. I also owe a large debt to Duncan Clark, who had the original idea for this book and steered it in its early days. James Alexander designed the book with exceptional flair, imagination and patience, and sourced many intriguing images, and Amanda Russell provided additional picture research and clearance.

I am hugely grateful to all those who agreed to be interviewed and generously shared their views and experience: Matthew Carter, Erik Spiekermann, Luc(as) de Groot, Zuzana Licko, Rodrigo Xavier Cavazos, Jim Parkinson, Margaret Calvert, Mark van Bronkhorst, Simon Learman, Tom Hingston, Paul Fenn, David Pearson, Paul Brand, Jonathan Barnbrook, Eiichi Kono, Cyrus Highsmith, Justin Callaghan, Tobias Frere-Jones and Aric Sigman. There are also many fine writers on type and typography whose work, listed in the bibilography and website sections, I have found useful; I would particularly like to guide readers towards books by Rick Poynor, Phil Baines and the late Justin Howes, and online to sites from Mark Simonson, David Earls and Yvos Potors.

Stephen Coles, Type Director at FontShop, and Nigel Roche, Librarian at the St Bride Library (a wondrous archive of printing history and graphic design), read the manuscript and corrected errors and misjudgements. Coles and FontShop also provided generous assistance with the licensing of many fonts in the book. Phil Baines and Catherine Dixon from Central Saint Martins read the manuscript with great care and insight, and made invaluable improvements. At the Department of Typography and Graphic Communication at Reading University, Martin Andrews and his colleagues were also immensely enthusiastic and supportive.

The Type Archive, as described in Chapter 17, is a priceless part of our national heritage, and long may it inspire and prosper. Thank you Sue Shaw for your patience, guidance and catering.

As always, the librarians at the London Library were the most efficient and friendly any writer could hope for.

Many other people contributed to this book, providing ideas, advice and inspiration. Thank you Bella Bathurst for being so wise. Thank you David Robson, Suzanne Hodgart, Jeff Woad, Tony Elliott, Lucy Linklater, Phil Cleaver and Andrew Bud for your knowledge and contacts, and Natania Jansz for your hospitality.

At United Agents, Rosemary Scoular and Wendy Millyard were, as ever, superbly sage companions.

Finally, this book would have been impossible without the love of Justine Kanter, JMT if ever there was.

Font and image credits

Font credits

The author and Profile Books are grateful to the following type foundries for allowing us to sample their fonts, and to FontShop for their help in making this possible: Bitstream, E&F, Emigre, Flat-it, Font Bureau, Font Font, Fontsmith, Fountain, GarageFonts, Gestalten, H&FJ, Jeremy Tankard Typography, LucasFonts, Monotype, MVB Fonts, Porchez Typofonderie, PSY/OPS, Richard Beatty, Samuelstype, Sudtipos, URW, Virus.

Fonts featured in this book include:

Academy Engraved; Aftershock Debris; Akzidenz Grotesk; Alte Schwabacher; Amanda; Ambroise Light; American Typewriter; Anglia Script; Antique Olive; Arial; Archer Hairline; MVB Aunt Mildred; Avalon; Avant Garde; Banco; Baskerville; ITC Bauhaus; Bell Centennial; Bembo; Bembo Book; Bliss; Blur; Bodoni; Bogart; Bollocks; Bookman; Braggadocio; ITC Brioso Pro Italic Display; FF Brokenscript; Brush Script; Bubble Bath; MVB Cafe Mimi; Calibri; Californian; Calliope; Calvert; Adobe Caslon; Caslon Old Style; Centaur; Century; Chalkduster; ITC Cheltenham; FF Chernobyl; Chicago; Clarendon; Colossalis; Comic Sans; Consolas; Crillee; Dante; De Vinne; Didot; DIN (Deutsche Industrie Norm); Dot Matrix; Ehrhardt; Electra; English 157; Erbar; Expanded Antique; Fairfield; Falafel; Fenice; Fette Fraktur; Flieger; Floydian; Franklin Gothic; Freight Sans Black; Frutiger; Futura; Galliard; Garamond; HT Gelateria; Geneva; Georgia; Gill Sans; Gotham; Goudy Oldstyle; Goudy Saks; Goudy Text; Grassy; Hands; Helvetica; Henrietta Samuels; Hounslow; Humana Serif Light; Impact; FF Info; FF Instantypes Dynamoe; Insignia; Jazz Let; Jesus Loves You; Joanna; Juniper; Kabel; Kiddo Caps; Kismet; Libra; FS Lola; Lombriz; London; Martini at Joe's; Melior; FF Meta; Minion; Mistral; Monster Droppings; Mr Eaves; Mrs Eaves; Naiv; Nebulae; Neue Helvetica; Neuland; Neuland Inline; New Baskerville; New York; Nimbus Sans Bold; ITC Officina Sans; ITC Officina Serif; Old Dreadful No 7; Old English; Ondine; Optima; Palatino; Papyrus; Parisine; Parkinson Condensed Bold; Parkinson Roman; Party Let;

Peignot; Perpetua; Playbill; Plexo; PowerStation; President; FF Profile; Quadraat; Regime; Reporter; Retablo; Riva; Rocky; Rotis; Sabon; San Francisco; Saphir; Scala; Scotch Roman; Scrawlz; Serpentine; Shelley; Souvenir; Stencil; Stoned; Swiss; Tahoma; TheMix; TheSans; TheSerif; Times New Roman; SG Today Sans Serif SH Ultra; Trajan; Transport; HT Trattoria; Trebuchet; FF Trixie; Underground; Univers; Universal; Vendôme; Verdana; Vivaldi; Vitrina; Walbaum; Zapf Dingbats; Zaphno; Zeppelin II and Zipper.

Image credits

p56 Courtesy of EasyJet; p61 © Zuzana Licko; p59 Photograph by Hope Harris; p62 © Zuzana Licko; p77 Cary Graphic Arts Collection, RIT, Rochester, NY; p75 Central Lettering Record at Central Saint Martins College of Art & Design; p92 © National Portrait Gallery, London; p99 Courtesy of MyFonts www.MyFonts.com; p96 The Granger Collection, NYC / TopFoto; p107 © National Portrait Gallery, London; p108 Central Lettering Record at Central Saint Martins College of Art & Design; p112 © Zuzana Licko; p113 Photograph by Alexander Blumhoff; p125 Photograph by Terrazzo (Flickr); p130 Photograph by David M Goehring (Flickr); p149 © National Portrait Gallery, London; p155 Courtesy of Margaret Calvert; p157 Photograph from the Cardozo Kindersley Workshop; p161 Courtesy of Tom Gourdie Jnr; p163 © Paula Perrins, Wychbury; p168 Photograph by Burn_the_asylum (Wikipedia); p171 © Javier Cañada; p185 Courtesy of Swiss Dots; p196 Courtesy of NASA/KSC; p199 GLC 00496.042. Courtesy of the Gilder Lehrman Institute of American History. Not to be reproduced without permission; p203 © William Barrett; p204 Cary Graphic Arts Collection, RIT, Rochester, NY; p218 courtesy of Pentagram. Freedom Tower Cornerstone, Michael Gericke, Designer; p236 © Andra Nelki/The Type Archive; ; p247 courtesy of David Pearson; p248 © Dutch Type Library; p257 © 2006 Paul Felton. Used by permission of Merrell Publishers Ltd; p263 © Neville Brody and Research Studios (some rights reserved); p259 © The Times, 2nd and 3rd October 1932/ nisyndication.com; p264 © Neville Brody and Research Studios (some rights reserved); p271 David Redfern/Getty Images; p300 Image courtesy of Mark Simonson; p301 Cary Graphic Arts Collection, RIT, Rochester, NY; p323 © Julia Kay, julia@studiojuliakay.com; p324 © Rick Banks / Face37; p329 © Thorsten Wulff.

Index

Figures in italics indicate images